# REA|
# 1u
# READING

## A BICYCLE JOURNEY
## AROUND THE WORLD

# TIM MILLIKIN

# READING TO READING

First Published in Great Britain 2020
Copyright © 2020 Tim Millikin

ISBN: 978-1-5272-7356-6

timmillikin.com

Dedicated to Grandad Ted, I miss you and
your adventurous soul

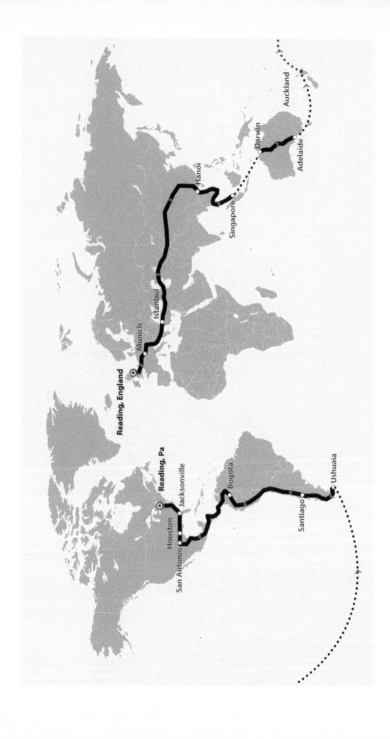

# Table of Contents

*Chapter One:*
# TENACITY

I crossed the border from Honduras to El Salvador with relative ease. It was a hot and humid 30 degrees Celsius as I entered El Salvador and it felt like riding through a clay oven. The dry and oppressive heat produced layers of sticky sweat which clung to my body and would not let go. I paid the ten US Dollars for my visa and was allowed to cross onto the other side of the steel barrier where I cycled straight up to a friendly woman selling pupusas, a cheap kind of pancake filled with cheese and potato, topped with salad and chilli sauce. It was three for a dollar! Bargain. I ordered my food and sat on the small plastic chair, smiling ear to ear, as the crunch of the salad, the warmth of the chilli and the comfort of the potato all mixed together to leave me feeling happy. I remembered how nervous I was about cycling through Honduras as I had heard so many negative things from other travellers before my arrival. Still, I had been treated kindly and offered safe passage by everyone I met. I hoped El Salvador would treat me the same.

My first day saw me cross late in the afternoon, so I decided to camp on some farmland about 10 kilometres from the border. The land was barren and rough, and the compacted ground crunched beneath my wheels. There was a trail I could follow and some trees I could hide behind, so I wheeled the bike onto the land and walked about 500 meters until I couldn't be seen from the road. I set up my camp and cooked a simple dish of rice and vegetables. For some reason, even though I had been camping like this for over two years, it always made me quite wary every time I entered a new country. Something about the unknown still had the ability to spook me. A kind of nervousness about being somewhere new, unsure about what was to come. Embracing this change and accepting this feeling of insecurity was what had made this trip so unique, so I pushed my fears aside and ventured forward with the secret smile of the wild camper.

To access this land, I had seen that the gate was open and taken this as a good sign. It is one of my rules to never open a gate or climb over a fence to reach a camping spot as it is clearly trespassing and will likely lead to trouble if found. It was my first day in El Salvador and I didn't want to get into bother around the border, so I made sure my camp spot was a long way from any human eyes. Another advantage of finding an open gate is that it is so much easier to push the bike onto open land than to force entry. That night, I set my tent up next to some trees which I hoped would give me some morning shade. Then I opened my can of Suprema beer, the local beer of El Salvador, to celebrate crossing the border. It had become something of a tradition which originated back when I first crossed into France on a ferry two years previously, since then, every time I crossed a border, I would celebrate by having a border crossing beer of the local flavour. This would give me a chance to reflect on the journey past and anticipate the road ahead. The beer of El Salvador went down well, and I soon fell asleep to the sound of silence.

The following morning I awoke around six. It had become routine for me to sleep when the sun went down and wake when the sun rose, as the natural light would shine directly into my tent, waking me with nature's natural rhythm. I awoke with anticipation of the day ahead, and after looking at my maps, I worked out that my day's goal was to get to the town of San Miguel in the afternoon and then head south towards the famous El Salvadorian coastal roads. El Salvador is a small country of about six million people, with the majority living in the capital city of San Salvador. This means there is a lot of traffic on neglected and congested roads headed towards the capital. This is a pattern seen throughout Central America and after cycling the unavoidable highways into Panama City, I had vowed to try and take the back roads where possible. I intended to cycle down the Pacific coast road where there should be less traffic and the tarmac potentially in better condition. Plus the natural ups and downs of a coastal road should provide a varied and more challenging ride. It is always better to take the difficult road; the harder the road, the bigger the reward. I ate my breakfast of banana porridge and packed up my camp before pushing my bike back onto the road to San Miguel. I wondered if I was able to buy San Miguel beer here and as the thoughts of the day ahead filled my mind, I carried on along the busy road towards the town.

The day was bright with an oppressive heat which was only matched by the intensity of the humidity. The lunchtime temperatures were getting close to 35 degrees which meant I had to drink a lot of water and take regular rest stops, but I enjoyed the challenge. I would much rather be cycling in the shorts and t-shirts required of hot weather than the multiple layers I wore while crossing high mountain passes of the Pamirs or Andes. I actually enjoy sweating, and I could feel my body and bike in total harmony as I cycled on quickly with my body adjusting to the Central American temperatures. The traffic was busy, but it didn't bother me too much. I was used to cycling alongside busy highways. I was so confident after cycling 40,000 kilometres without a significant incident that I carried my helmet clipped to the back of my panniers and rode with my headphones in. The traffic passed to my left as I cycled close to the right-hand side of the road and although no cycle lanes were provided the road seemed wide enough to accommodate me and the traffic safely. It was only the potholes that occasionally required me to position myself more centrally on the road and in the path of the traffic, something I did not enjoy doing!

I stopped by the small town of Santa Rosa de Lima and stocked up on supplies for lunch. My lunch usually consisted of banana sandwiches and I would eat this almost every day.

The taste, the price, and the fact that it really filled me up meant it was the perfect lunch for a long distance cyclist. My favourite type of bread to use was a crusty roll, but these were harder to find in Central America so often I would have a tortilla or sweet white bread. In Santa Rosa, I purchased a loaf of cheap sweet bread, bananas, some vegetables and a packet of biscuits, and after a quick sit down in the main square, I set off again towards San Miguel.

I stopped and veered onto a little patch of land for lunch somewhere just past the township of Jocaro. I sat there under the shade of a tree, lying back onto the arid ground and relaxing before eating my meal. I was tired and content, but the midday heat was sapping my energy so I nearly drank all of my water. I would have to stop in the next town. I remember feeling quite concerned about this as I didn't really want to have to stop again. I lay there listening to a podcast by Adam Buxton and Romesh Ranganathan talking about hip hop before packing up, popping my headphones in and hitting the road once again. I was looking forward to getting to San Miguel. I wanted to have a cold beer and find a relaxing shady camp spot.

The next thing I remember is the sound of brakes behind me and looking back to see a blue pickup just a few feet away from my back wheel and coming closer. The only thoughts that went through my head were "Oh shit!" Although it was more prolonged more like "Ohhhhhhhhhhhhhhhhhhhhhhh shit!" And then nothing. A constant blackness over this period which I have never been able to regain. All I remember is coming to on the side of the road, looking up and seeing a policeman in a smart blue uniform who was standing next to a woman wearing casual clothes. My head hurt, and I knew I was in trouble, I opened my mouth, and the only word that came out was "Hospital?"

I have no memory of being hit. I do not know how I landed or what happened to my bike, my possessions. I do not know if I flew over the car or just landed in a heap. I do not know if any other vehicles stopped or passed me by or how long I was unconscious for. The doctors told me later that this is a typical sign of a serious concussion and that memory loss often follows a head injury. I only know that whoever called the police could be the person that had saved my life, and I do not know who that person is. I wish I could thank them and tell them how grateful I am. Was it the woman I saw when I came around, or some passing driver? I will never know. Thank you, kind person, whoever you are.

The policeman put me straight into the back of his police car, and with sirens and lights on, he drove me straight to the main hospital. I knew it must be serious if they were not waiting for the ambulance. I remember being in the police car and looking down and seeing my t-shirt covered in blood, I felt beat up and dizzy. In my confused state, I managed to find a small bag of water in the side pocket of the car door, and I opened it to drink it to quench my thirst, but as I was drinking it, the policeman took it away from me. I was confused and annoyed as to why he would take away my water, but I quickly passed out again and didn't come to until I was in the hospital and on the way to the operating theatre.

Although I had gone through serious trauma, I felt calm and unworried. Whenever something serious happens, I always seem to gain an air of calm, and this was no exception. I knew it was best to let the doctors and nurses take over, and I wanted to help them do their jobs and put me right. I knew I was in a hospital, a safe place, and had this feeling everything would be alright. I felt that either my body was aware of the injuries I had sustained, or possibly my ignorance of my injuries combined with my positive attitude helped calmed me down. Or maybe it was just the drugs administered! Still, in any case, I entered the operating room without any fear. I was introduced to the doctors who would do the surgery on my head, and as they looked down at me with their gowns and masks on, I said to them "I don't have any insurance," and to my relief, their reply was "Don't worry, we have public healthcare here – there's nothing to pay!"

A huge weight was lifted as I did not have much money left. Relieved, I then asked the doctor to take a picture of my injuries which he did before I passed out and they operated on my head.

I awoke the next day in a hospital bed with bandages around my forehead and over both knees. I was being administered drugs every few hours via a drip, and I spent most of that day sleeping. The doctor came in to see me, and luckily he spoke good English. "We have sewed up your forehead and you have had a bad concussion." He told me "I am worried about your brain swelling and we want to keep you in for a week to monitor you and take some scans."

My skull had no fractures, and I had no broken bones. I had, however, sprained both ankles, my knees were damaged but not broken, and my head would scar over but recover. If my brain had no swelling, he told me I could go home in a week, maybe. I felt this was good news, as it meant that I was going to be alright. At the time, I did not know the potential risk of brain damage. Later, I would learn that had my brain swelled, it could have caused a cerebral oedema, which means the swelling cuts off the oxygen to my brain and could have killed me. But unaware of the danger, I thanked the doctor for his time and went back to sleep.

The hospital itself was a large concrete building in the middle of San Miguel. I was on the third floor, in a room with three other beds connected in parallel to another room with four beds. The walls were painted a cream colour and the beds covered with white sheets. Each bed was connected to an IV and a monitor. It was simple but comfortable. I was the only foreigner in the two rooms, and although my Spanish was at a decent level, it was tough to communicate with the people around me, especially after my head had taken a knock. I soon found out that the man in the bed opposite me was in the hospital because his finger had been cut off with a machete in a bar fight. Next to me was a boy no older than 16 who had also been in a car accident whilst riding his bike, as was another man in the final bed. They had both broken their spines, and were potentially paralysed. Watching them unable to move the lower halves of their bodies made me thankful how lucky I had been: things could have been much, much worse.

I spent the first few days in a recovery routine: drugs, sleep, food, repeat. The doctors would make the rounds at 5 a.m. to check that everyone was OK each morning. This was the only time I got to speak English and get updates on my situation. After about three days, I was starting to feel stronger, but the downside of this was that I was beginning to feel really lonely. I was in a hospital in another country after being hit by a car, and nobody knew I was there. Life was going on outside, and here I was stuck, unable even to call home as everything I owned was left on the side of the road after the crash. I wanted to scream, to speak English, to run away but was unable to do anything. Food was served at 9 a.m., midday and 4 p.m. meaning I was starving by nightfall and then even more so in the morning. This was much harder mentally than actually being hit physically by the car, and I cried often. I felt so isolated and started to become jealous of the other patients in the ward who had their families around them.

What was I doing in the middle of Central America while my friends and family back home carried on without me? Thoughts of selfishness about my travels would not leave me and depression was starting to seep in. I felt that the people around me were laughing at me, unable to speak Spanish, the stupid gringo who rides his bike everywhere without family or relationships. I just wanted to tell someone what happened. I was so desperately lonely, that when the embassy called (I found out later the police had found my passport and reported my crash), I broke down and asked to go home. The embassy agreed to call my parents who I could only imagine were shocked to receive the news. It must be a parent's worst nightmare to get a call from the British Embassy telling them that their son is in hospital in El Salvador!

After speaking with my parents, I felt better, but I knew I had a big decision to make: to stay or go. That day all I wanted was to go home. I knew I had some thinking to do, and since I could hardly walk, I had the time to think. I did not sleep much that night. Even though I wanted to go home, I could not shake the burning stubbornness in my head. I had come this far. Could I really give up with only 6000 kilometres to go? Could I go home and finish this another day? What would people think about me quitting? What would I think? Did I even have a working bike at this point?

I knew I had some soul searching to do, so I stalled any decision until the doctors gave me positive news about any possible brain swelling. My head felt fine at this point, and I had no headaches or blurred vision which was a good sign. The following day I went for a CAT scan. I laid down and was inserted head first into the machine. It was an alien experience, and I felt claustrophobic and nervous as the machine whirred and took me in. A few hours later, after a drug-induced sleep back at my bed, a young doctor came to visit me. He wore a white coat and had a clipboard in his hand. He was short with a kind face, and he showed me the results of the CAT scan. He first showed me the X-ray and then moved on to photographs of my brain. It was weird to see my brain represented on a single translucent page. I checked for defects and saw none, and he confirmed that my brain was undamaged. I was relieved, although in a way I had kind of expected this result. I think my body knew this already, and the report felt more like confirmation rather than positive news. It seems I either have a thick skull or a small brain as I had escaped with a minor miracle. No adverse effects, battered and bruised but not a single bone was broken. My head was fine, although the team wanted me to stay another three days for further checks. It was then that I knew I would survive this, and there was a possibility I could continue my journey. Although next time, my helmet would sit firmly on my head rather than being clipped to the back of the bike.

Later that morning the doctor came in and let me use his mobile phone to Skype home. It must have shocked my family to actually see me, sat up in a hospital bed with a bandage around my head. Emotions poured to the surface after being in hospital for five days. To be able to tell them I would be OK meant a lot to both me and them. I told them I had not made a decision about what to do, and in their supportive way, they said that they would help me no matter what decision I came to. I had cycled 40,000 kilometres by this point, and that is a long way on a bicycle.

The following day I was feeling stronger and determined. I woke up and began to move out of the bed. I pulled myself out of the ward by holding on to the wall. My legs hurt, and my muscles felt cramped and tight. My ankles were swollen, and although it was only a short walk, after five days stuck immobile in my hospital bed, it represented progress. I started walking a little bit more, and although I was still not allowed out of the hospital, I was walking up and down the hallway. I was feeling confident at my little progress, when six days after I arrived, the British Ambassador rang again to check on me. "Thank you," I said, "But I feel like I'm going to be alright. I'm not going home, I'm going to finish this trip. I've only got another 6000 kilometres after all!" He congratulated me on my decision and added "If you come to San Salvador, make sure you come and see me at the embassy." I said a warm-hearted thank you to the Ambassador, and with the spirit of the British adventurers of a time gone by, he wished me all the luck in the world. I was going to continue this big bike ride. It was my aim to cycle from Reading, England to Reading, Pennsylvania, and I was so close now. It would only take a further five months.

Eight days after my accident, I checked out of the hospital. Although still in no condition to ride my bike, it was a relief to be able to leave, and I said many a thank you to the hospital staff and doctors who looked after me and treated me with nothing but kindness. I was a stranger in their hospital, and their care was excellent. Warmth radiated off the grey walls as I thanked each member of staff individually. When it was time to leave, the nurse had to cut off the stitches in my forehead and kept apologising since the scissors were blunt. They would tug and pull at the stitches rather than cut, but I did not mind; I understood and was grateful for their care and attention during my time there.

On leaving the hospital, one of the nurses managed to get the police to come down and deliver some of my belongings. I was told there that it was a hit and run incident and he could only give me some of my possessions back since the case was under investigation. I was angry. I had often sat in the hospital wondering how the driver was doing: were they hurt or even in the same hospital, was their car damaged? But instead, the bastard had simply driven away, not even stopping to call the police. The police tried to calm me down by telling me it is typical in El Salvador as if the driver was caught, they would go to prison. I was not reassured and felt tricked; the idea that this was a hit and run had not entered my head at all until this point. The police asked if I had seen the number plate, but as I was hit from behind and had no memory of the crash, even if I had seen it at the time, this information was now lost.

I was, however, happy to receive my wallet and passport along with some clothes as it meant I was able to check into a hotel in town and have some of my freedom back. One of my main frustrations with being in the hospital was not being allowed out, so it was with great relief I was able to leave. In one last gracious gift from the San Miguel hospital, the nurse then offered to drive me into the town where I was able to find a hotel with English TV and Wi-Fi for just seven dollars a night. This was perfect as it meant I was able to rest and recover for as long as I needed and not have to worry about the cost of the hotel on my dwindling finances. The hotel was run by a small team of local men and was part-hotel part-brothel where you were able to rent the room by the hour! I often wonder what the men made of the strange man who hobbled in on crutches to take a room for the week, but at least the sheets were cleaned daily!

My recovery in the hotel took a further week, but it was great to be able to speak to friends and family back home, all of who were very supportive of my plans to continue. It really was touching to read such uplifting messages from everyone who had sent me support. Thank you to everyone who wished me well, to those who were able to send a little cash to help me get back on the road. It made me see that my friends and family were behind me, and that this journey wasn't the selfish endeavour to see the world alone as I had started to feel in my hospital bed. Each message, phone call and donation gave me confidence to continue and filled my heart with love for the community that I had so missed when I was in the hospital.

I was particularly grateful to my friends Kenneth and Marie, both tall, blonde Danes with blue eyes and kind hearts, whom I had cycled with in Bolivia and Peru. They were in the north of the country and came back from their own bike trip to stay with me for a few days at the brothel hotel. It made me feel normal again to go out to the local restaurants and drink a beer together. They both shared my positive outlook on life, and it was great to catch up and share stories of our adventures. Hearing about what they had been up to since we last had ridden together made me hungry for the road.

To be able to get back on the road, the first thing I needed to do was collect my bike from the police station back in Jacaro, where I had my crash. I took the bus back there as per the instructions from the policeman at the hospital, but once I arrived, I was told I could not collect everything until I had completed all the paperwork. The provincial police station in Jacaro was a small wooden outbuilding and did not have a computer, meaning I would have to visit another town 30 kilometres away! Luckily the police were able to give me a lift, and it only took about two hours for the paperwork to be completed. The police here really looked after me, and we all shared a lunch of tortillas and refried beans, before I was reunited with all my belongings. I looked over everything, and it was all there. I was so happy. The only thing I had lost were my glasses and my phone which had likely flown into a bush somewhere. Even my little souvenirs had been collected at the scene, which must have taken some time.

My bike was a different matter. The frame was broken in two places. The rear rack was twisted into the rear wheel which was also buckled. The pedals were damaged along with the crank arm, and the saddle post was bent. It looked as though the bike had taken most of the impact instead of me, for which I am eternally grateful. Unable to cycle or even push my belongings I asked the police if they were able to give me a lift back to San Miguel. "We're sorry, but our car is needed elsewhere," I was told "but follow us, we'll help you hitch a lift back to town."

We drove the bike down the small cobbled streets to the main road. It only took a few minutes as we passed small buildings with confused locals staring at the passing tourist with his head bandaged up. Inside the police car were three policemen and myself, everyone under thirty-five. We drove slowly and silently, with a sense that we were all on a mission. As we approached the junction of the main road, we all got out and they helped me unload all my equipment onto the side of the road. It was a heavy load and we dumped it all in a pile, me trying to make my baggage look as small as possible. But my worries that passing drivers would not want to stop were soon put to rest as all three policemen strode into the middle of the road to pull over a passing pick up truck with their shotguns on display! The driver quickly stopped but it turned out he was going another way. Soon, a small white pickup stopped for my armed friends, and I was told to jump onto the back while they handed me all my baggage and broken bicycle. The family inside looked friendly, as if this kind of thing happened all the time, and we drove off towards the town of San Miguel as I waved goodbye to the policemen from the back of the truck.

The drive was short and only took about twenty minutes as we passed the main roads, but unfortunately, the driver did not know where I wanted to be dropped off, so missed the turning to the town. He had to turn around a few times as I shouted directions from my phone through his window, in a language and accent he did not understand. I was ground growing vegetables, but quickly we both got fitter, and as our muscles grew strong it was no problem to wake up at 5 a.m. and walk straight onto the fields to begin a seven or eight-hour day.

Picking vegetables is actually very similar to long-distance cycling: You start out unfit and the only way to get fitter is by repetition and by sticking to your plan even if at times you want to quit. After just two weeks of cycling or fruit picking, you are as fit as you need to be to pick vegetables or cycle across a county. Nick, realising this work was not for him, left after the first month. I continued to work as I needed the money to fund my travels. The days went quickly, and soon my three-month contract was complete, and I never wanted to see another courgette again.

As I left the farm, alone with all my possessions loaded into my backpack, I headed to the bus station for a mini Australian adventure which would see me visit the back-packer strongholds of Brisbane, Airlie Beach, 1770 and Cairns. I enjoyed my bus-hopping journey, but I could not shake the feeling that something was missing. I was going from hostel, to bar, to bus, to hostel. Although this was fun, I was just spending my time getting drunk with other western travellers and not seeing anything outside of that. I was missing Australia's beautiful landscapes, and its rich and diverse culture. All the while spending a fortune and losing all my fitness from my farm work.

Was this really travelling or just another way to avoid work? Was this any different from the working world as I hopped around the country on various forms of motorised transport and got drunk in different bars? I was dissatisfied, and my soul was calling for a change. I wanted a new direction and did not know where to look, until one day while sitting alone on a Greyhound bus I had an epiphany. Maybe I could see Australia by bike... I could cycle around the country and live in a tent. I could be truly independent, save money, and keep my levels of fitness up. It would be difficult, I didn't know where to start, and I didn't know the way. But Hell, if I could cycle around Australia... Maybe I could cycle home. I wrote in my notebook, which I still have to this day, the rough plans of a cycle ride from Australia to England via South-East Asia, China, Central Asia and Europe. I estimated that the journey would take perhaps nine months and I wrote that this would be my re-birth, a new beginning in my life. I was super excited and had just unwittingly written the blueprint which would give me a whole new philosophy for life.

At this time, I did not have any cycling experience and had never cycled further than perhaps 10 miles back in my youth. I did, however, enjoy cycling and had commuted by bike both at University and while I worked in London. I knew that when I rode a bike, I was happy, and felt a level of freedom which I never felt on a bus or in a car. At this time, I did not know that there was a thing called cycle-touring, and my idea came entirely from a desire to be free rather with physical exhaustion, hardship, and often no real under-standing of what I am taking on. I forget not everyone thinks like me, and for this reason, Finola was uncertain about such a big trip.

"What are we going to do about water," she said, "or food, it's going to be big distances between towns and we can't cycle in the day, it's too hot."

"We can stop in the midday heat. Swim perhaps," I countered. "Let's get the bikes, then we can see how far and fast we can go. Then we can make a proper plan!"

There is nothing like the fun of preparing for a big cycle trip, especially when working with budget constraints. We had very little money and were starting from scratch so needed to buy everything, so we knew that our preparation had to be guided by this. We had to buy second-hand bikes and make our panniers out of whatever we could find. We trawled eBay and Gumtree, and I managed to find a bike seller in Cairns who specialised in second-hand bikes. I contacted him and went over to his garage in the east of the city. To my surprise, he had more than 50 bikes all ready to go with tags on. We discussed my plans, and he recom-mended a Giant Boulder Bike with 26" wheels, V-Brakes and a steel rear rack. I was sold and bought my new bike for $100AUD, which was about £50 at the time. A bargain, I thought until Finola purchased her bike for just $10AUD, which she found in a second-hand garage sale, in perfect working order. It is surprising what you can find if you look around. If you only have a little bit of money, you only spend a little bit of money, and you have to get creative. To go alongside the bikes we decided to make something to carry our backpacks and gear, so we cable-tied two milk crates to the rack on the back of each bike and simply put our bags in them. Any other equipment we would put in baskets on the front of the bikes. This simple home-made system did work, but it was very back heavy, and the backpacks would swing left and right as we cycled. This became very dangerous, especially when cornering as sometimes the packs would just fall out if not tied down well enough!

After working out that this new set up would simply be too slow, we decided that we would not be able to cover the 100 kilometres per day each day to reach the music festival. I was quite disappointed by this as I really wanted the challenge and felt if we just cycled enough hours each day the distance would do itself, but Finola was still feeling unsure, and did not want to have to push herself to the limit every day. This was a journey about seeing places rather than a test of our cycling abilities, so we agreed to take the train from Cairns to Noosa. This was a 15-hour train journey and took away about 1300 kilometres, leaving us 700 kilometres to cover by bike, which was much more manageable in the two weeks we had remaining until the festival began. That meant we would arrive at the festival on Christmas-Eve and could spend Christmas together at the festival site, which we thought would be an exciting and romantic place to celebrate.

Our train pulled into the station at Noosa, a beautiful whitewashed beach town on the sunshine coast of Southern Queensland. A place with golden sand on one side and wild forest with koala bears on the other. A great place to start. We cycled 20 kilometres to the beach, and it was hard work. I think we were both unprepared in fitness levels and with bikes so unstable we could not go at a steady speed. It had been a wise decision to get the train. If we had managed only an average speed of 10 kilometres per hour, we could not have made the festival and could have been in some real danger due to the heat and isolation of Northern Queensland. Sometimes the decisions you make at the time hurt. I did not want to get the train as it was both expensive, and I felt we would shorten our adventure, but once I could see the reality of what our first day of bike touring was like, then I knew we had made the right choice. We camped out in Noosa that night and the next day began heading south towards Brisbane. Neither of us slept well as it was our first night wild camping and we argued about where and when to camp, how to set up the tent and if we should not have any lights on inside the tent in case someone came past! This was only day one, and we were already fighting.

I put this down to the exhaustion and stress caused by the first day and also due to us not getting much sleep the night before on the train. The following day, the optimism was back in the air as we made breakfast and coffee overlooking the large expensive houses over the estuary. We had views of their beautiful homes whilst the rich occupants had views of two smelly cyclists cooking on their gas stove. We cycled south to explore the rest of Noosa before heading off towards Mooloolaba. It was flat with a light tailwind to guide us south. We stopped for lunch and felt the heat on our faces as we no longer had the cool breeze provided by our movement. To cool down we decided to go swimming. The sea was calm and blue and the beach covered only with fine, sharp, hot sand, with not another person in sight. Cooling our hot bodies in the pleasant sea reminded us that this was an adventure to do and see things as much it was about cycling. It was idyllic and gave me my first taste of truly independent travel with the ability to just stop where we wanted and go swimming in the Coral Sea, rather than rushing past on an expensive and crowded bus.

We continued in this vein, and one of the things I think we both realised was how vulnerable and open you can be when touring on a bike. We would continually meet people and receive offers of help or places to stay. We were open to their offers, and saying yes meant we were able to meet and talk with the local people in a way that was impossible when I was travelling by bus and staying in hostels. We cycled into Woodford for the music festival on the 24th December. We set up camp and drank wine to celebrate. We had made it, our first cycle trip, and we had learned so much so quickly. We had seen places we would not have seen otherwise, we had got fitter and met interesting people along the way. We slept on beaches, under bushes and in peoples homes. It was a real adventure, and gave us both our first taste of what authentic travel can be.

It was not all happiness however, as while the cycle touring itself had been amazing, I felt it had put a strong downer on our relationship. In one way it brought us together, but it was also one of the first times when I felt we were two people on different journeys rather than on a shared journey together. It is hard to spend all your time together as you have to on a bike tour; relationships need constant work and communication, but it is far easier to just put your head into the sand and ignore any problems especially when you are tired and hungry. We started to argue a lot towards the end of this first trip, often about the little things like what to eat and how to put the tent up. I had wanted to test myself physically. I wanted to cycle further and see more, whereas Finola wanted to explore her spiritual side. This polar opposite viewpoint was the root cause of many of our problems, and it culminated at the festival where I often felt like an outsider, and resulted in us spending our time with different people. I was on a different path; I wanted to explore, but not spiritually. I had little interest in exploring energy and meditation when I felt that my eyes had so much more to see.

I left the festival early alone and went to visit some friends 45 minutes away. I felt more comfortable in this setting. It was a hard realisation, but as I returned to the festival after a few days away, I could see that Finola and I were now different people. We still loved each other and decided to continue travelling together but not by bicycle. Our journey had been about reaching the destination of the music festival but what we had learned was so much more important. I think it scared us both, as the truth was thrust to the surface that perhaps our relationship was not as stable as we thought and the celebration of reaching the festival became a realisation that we were better apart.

To both heal and forget, we sold our bikes and belongings and bought a car and continued to travel and work around Australia, and in this manner, we both got on much better. We hiked the natural parks of the West Coast, swam with whale sharks and drove from Perth to Darwin with fewer arguments. Perhaps we were just more rested. But I think that travelling by bike gives you a certain clarity of togetherness and sometimes that clarity is scary and uncertain. By travelling in a more conventional way we were able to forget our problems. It was a good first test, we had learnt so much about bicycle travel and each other and perhaps next time would be more successful.

After a year of travel, Finola's visa was running out, and we decided to return home to England. We had very little money left at this point and the idea to cycle home from Australia was shelved, but the concept and original idea stuck with me. The ability to be free, to cycle long distances and stop and rest wherever I wanted. To see all the places in between the bus stops. To cycle home at that moment would have been wrong, but the seed had been planted. I knew I wanted to cycle a long distance and see the world. I have a natural curiosity and an inability to sit still.

We returned from Australia, rented an apartment and got office jobs, but it all felt too safe. The fire, the burning desire inside of me had not gone away: I wanted to explore. I wanted to cycle around the world.

*Chapter Four:*

# THE BEGINNING

We came up with the plan to cycle from Reading, UK to Reading, USA, simply as a way to bookend the trip. I thought it would be a fun little gimmick to have an identical start and finish point rather than just heading around the world. This actually helped on the road to have a target and gave me something to aim towards. People would always ask me why I was finishing in Reading, Pennsylvania but it was merely because it had the same name as my home town and being just 100 miles south of New York, I thought it would make an excellent place to end the trip.

Planning a bike trip is much more than just working out a start and finish points. Although I had a rough route in my mind, it made it much clearer to just go and buy a big map and actually draw a line of our proposed route. I stuck the map on the wall, marked the start in Reading, UK and went east. I drew my line across Europe, Turkey and Central Asia, across China and South-east Asia, going south to Australia and New Zealand and then worked my way back from the bottom of Argentina and headed north again through South and Central America before coming to rest in Reading, PA. Just seeing this line helped me put the trip in perspective, and I was able to see how much ground I had to cover. It helped me be clearer when telling people about my journey and gave me something to work towards. A simple line became much more than that. It reflected my hopes and dreams for this trip, and it became the framework for my adventure, giving me the focus to go to work daily and earn the savings I needed.

Finola and I worked modest jobs in England. She worked in a call centre for the water board taking phone calls from angry customers who had issues with their water, and I worked as a travel agent with Flight Centre, meaning I got to help people plan their own travel stories. This also gave me the scope to work on my own bike travel plans as I would spend the day looking up holiday destinations for people, and this, in turn, inspired me. I think most people who work in the travel industry have a yearning to go away and I was no different. Still, I did not tell my employers about my travel plans straight away as this was my little secret, and I figured I had another 18 months of work before we would have enough savings to begin.

Finola and I put together a plan where we would open a bank account, and each put £250 away a month, meaning that in 18 months we would have around £9000. This would give us a budget of just over £6 per day each. I felt this should be enough money for two people to cycle for two years, which is how long I thought that the journey would take at the time. We initially decided to leave on 1st April 2015, as this would mean going in spring which is a mild time for Europe, but also meant we would reach the mountains of Central Asia before they became impassable in winter. After some serious deliberation we decided to put the trip back a month to give us an extra month of saving. This way we could cycle for longer overall and we calculated we would still be in Kyrgyzstan around October when the passes would be cold, but just about passable. We landed on the 1st May 2015 as the departure date.

As in Australia, the bikes had to be purchased on a budget as we did not have the money to buy expensive kit, and wanted to spend our money on the adventure rather than the gear. We decided to get cheap, simple, second-hand bikes which were easy to repair and reliable. This strategy had worked well for us in Australia, and we spent our time trying to figure out how to get the best bikes for the least money. For me this meant buying the frame second hand for £90, before adding all the components from my old mountain bike. This allowed me to construct the bike exactly how I wanted with the added bonus of teaching me how to repair it if anything ever broke on the road.

I was lucky that in the run-up to our departure, a community project called the Reading Bicycle Kitchen opened. This was a community space where people could come in and repair their bikes using the available tools under the supervision of volunteers. I joined up to both help and learn all about how to repair and fix bikes. The

Bicycle Kitchen was able to bring in some money by repairing and then selling off donated bikes, so I had the opportunity to work on many different bikes and frames and increase my knowledge tenfold. This knowledge was so important as it meant I was able to then fix and repair problems without having to visit expensive bike shops and I would be much more self-sufficient if anything ever broke and I was hundreds of miles away from help.

Finola's bike was once again an amazing find from eBay, costing just £120 for a bike in her size that was ready-made and needed no work. Both bikes, in the end, turned out to be extremely reliable and proved to be a worthy investment of our time as we had more money to spend on the adventure. Now we had the bikes, we bought all our gear from second-hand retailers, and started to prepare for the day we would leave. As time got closer the perceptions in both our heads and others shifted. People stopped asking if we were really going and instead just wished us good luck. A sense of nervousness and excitement came over us as we had a big leaving party at the Reading beer festival, and it was great to share the experience with our friends and family. Originally we had planned to go the day after the beer festival, but Finola rightly suggested this might be a bit tough with the emotion and added hangovers, so we changed our start date to 5th May. A wise choice, as with our sore heads the next morning, I do not think we would have got very far!

It was the day of our departure, and we were all packed up and ready to go. I had never ridden my bike fully loaded until the day we left, and it was a bit of a shaky start before I found my balance, but I soon had the hang of it. It was also the first time I had worn clip-in shoes. Apparently, these maximise the efficiency of your pedal strokes, but all I found was that it increased your chances of falling over at traffic lights. I fell three times that day because I was unable to unclip when I stopped. After that, the shoes were quickly re-homed in a nearby charity shop.

We left my house after having a quick photo before my friend Matt turned up in his full Lycra cycling gear! He looked professional with his tight clothes while we were in shorts and t-shirts. Matt cycled with us into town, to the starting point which was to be outside the Reading Bicycle Kitchen on Jackson's Corner, Reading. All our friends and family met us there for photos and teary goodbyes, before we hopped back on the bikes and turned, waved goodbye for the final time and pushed the pedals on their first rotation on the new wheel of life. We were off! It was a great moment, as it marked the moment in which we both changed the direction of our lives. We had just left everything and everybody behind as we headed for the rest of the world. My parents were crying, and only looking back now can I reflect how it must have felt for them to see us ride away to go around the world. They must have been worried and concerned, as we ventured into a world unknown to them. My emotional state was one of excitement. I had dreamed of this moment for over two years, and now here I was cycling slowly under the extra weight. Everything I owned was with me, and I was sharing this adventure with the person I loved. We had made the decisions and sacrifices to get us to this point, and now as we turned the pedals, we were the masters of our story. We had the freedom to write each chapter and make the decisions of what to do, where to go and who to spend our time with. I waved for a final time before turning the corner and pushed forward towards places I had only ever dreamed about.

*Chapter Five:*
# CHANGE

London marked the destination on our first day, and we had planned to have a second leaving meal with Finola's auntie and uncle who lived in North London right at the top of Muswell Hill. We were due to arrive there around six, but since we had never ridden loaded bikes before and we got lost several times, we were two hours late. We finally arrived just before eight, as it was getting dark and after pushing all the way up the very steep Muswell Hill. It was great to see everyone, but we were both exhausted, and we were fast asleep by 10. That first day we covered 100 kilometres, which was significantly more than either of us had ever cycled before. We woke up sore but excited for the next day's challenge; we had another 100 kilometres to cover to get us to the Airbnb we had booked in the town of Faversham.

We were quite hesitant to camp in England since neither of us had wild-camped before, so we booked accommodation in advance to help us to become accustomed to riding longer distances and being away from home. What we did not count on was that during that weekend, England was battered by hurricane-like gales, and we regularly rode past shop fronts with their tables and benches blown over, reflecting our own collapsing spirits. We pressed onwards into the wind, which was trying to hold us back; the final hurdle to overcome was mother nature as she blew down everything around us. This was our first experience of serious headwind. We slogged and shouted our way through the wind and through the undulating British countryside, both of us at times just wanting to stop, but as we had the accommodation booked, it left us little choice but to keep going. We were getting frustrated and weary with our slow progress, but we finally arrived tired and hungry, long after dark. This early in the trip, it was an uphill struggle each day to cover 100 kilometres without a GPS and with the wind in our faces, but we were still enjoying it. We had not booked the ferry to take us to France, so at least we knew we would be able to arrive into Dover at any time the following day as the ferries ran every two hours.

The final descent into Dover was fun as we rode past all the stationary lorries queuing to enter the port. We felt triumphant as we had reached our first milestone and were excited to be able to soon cycle in a new country. We booked the first available ferry which left at 8 p.m. and would take four hours, arriving in France at midnight. We celebrated by having the first of (what would become) our traditional border crossing beers on the ferry halfway across the English Channel.

We arrived in France, tired and slightly tipsy, in the pitch black night on fully-laden bikes which we had only ridden for the first time three days ago. Our final challenge was to navigate to the cheap hotel we had booked somewhere to the east of the port, using just a few printed paper maps.

Planning is important, but it is more important to leave than it is to plan extensively. Most problems can be sorted out on the road. In our planning however, we had given little, if any, thought to navigation, and this was a significant oversight for us both. We were not up to speed with the latest technology and did not realise it was possible to download GPS applications or use mapping software. We carried paper maps printed from Google, printing off different levels of scale which we would use to navigate in larger towns. We also had a compass, so we could in theory just travel south-east and we should reach Turkey or thereabouts! This was naive, but to our credit, we managed to navigate from Reading to France using this method, and although it was not easy, it was possible.

It was dark and we scanned our maps but could not find the hotel. We looked around for signs and quickly found that we had printed maps of an entirely different French port! I had presumed we would arrive into the main port of Dunkirk, but instead, we were somewhere five kilometres to the east, so it was impossible to find our way. We tried for about half an hour, but we were both tired and stressed so decided we needed to sleep and therefore camp. As we were away from the main port, the area was quiet, and we quickly managed to find a piece of grass where we could wild camp. We found this spot in the corner of what we believed to be a small park and went about setting up the tent. At this moment, we realised we did not know how to put the fly-sheet on as we had never practised beforehand and in frustration I broke my headlamp. With no torchlight to continue, we decided to just sleep under the mesh and hope it did not rain. At around 6 a.m. we awoke to the rain! As we stirred, eyes half-open, we were confronted by an irate French farmer, who told us in no uncertain terms in his angriest French to get off his land. Neither of us could speak French, so though we tried to explain our situation and ask for directions. He spoke no English, so we thought it best to pack up as quickly as we could and leave before he got angrier. He drove off as we packed and I am sure he most likely recounted the story of finding two travellers in a partially erected tent, in the pouring rain on his farm to all his friends later on.

We cycled around until we found the main town and then were able to ask at the local boulangerie where the hotel was. We were not too far off, but we would never have found it at night. The hotel told us we would have to book another night as we were technically no-shows from the night before, but they would give us the room for just £25. We agreed and checked into the smallest room in the hotel. We slept in the small plastic room before heading to the local supermarket and buying a bottle of red wine, some Brie, a baguette and a pot of pate. This was our first day in France after all, and after battling hurricanes, deadlines, cycling 270 kilometres and getting woken up by the rain and an angry French farmer I think we deserved it!

Cycling through Europe was easier than we first thought, as the countries went by quickly and we were able to make good progress. We were now making our way across northern France, and in no time we had crossed France and entered Belgium. In Europe, due to the Schengen Agreement, there are no physical borders between EU countries making the crossing between countries fast and easy. Upon arrival in Belgium, we decided to head towards Bruges and see the iconic and romantic town. Plus it was an excuse for me to eat mussels and chips, and quote as many lines from the film *In Bruges* as I could! "I want a normal gun for a normal person!"

We did not stay overnight in Bruges as the accommodation here was too costly, so we wild camped on the outskirts of the town and then returned in the morning for a coffee. It was great to be able to just swing by the tourist places as if we were locals. Bruges was full of tourists, and you could see why as people sat around the open piazza, under the shadow of the clock tower, chatting, laughing and watching the world go by. Still, we didn't fit this mould, either in appearance or mindset. I prefer wide-open nature with no one around, but if you are passing somewhere which is famous then you should try and pop in. The fact that we were able to visit the town without paying for accommodation made us both feel quite smug, and we were slowly getting used to wild camping.

A few days later, we cycled down a tree-lined gravel road to set up camp, adjacent to a large and empty field. As we lay quietly in our tent, we awoke to hear snorting and galloping behind us. Goosebumps rose up our arms as we sprung awake, worried that we were going to be attacked by a headless horseman. I did the gentlemanly thing and risked my life to look out of the tent and to my relief saw just a few horses right behind us in the previously vacant field. Wild camping takes some getting used to: when you spend your time sleeping in homes and even campsites, it takes time to make the mental shift needed to sleep out in the wild, but with time and practice, you soon become accustomed to sleeping anywhere. Sleeping in the wild is far more fun than hotels, which soon become boring and feel soulless. Wild camping is exciting, leads to chance encounters and gives you the ultimate freedom to sleep anywhere. To be able to stop wherever you want provides you with true empowerment over your trip and the decisions that you make. You need vulnerability and trust to go camping without permission, but doing so can also give you real confidence. Only by wild camping can you truly shed your fear of the unknown, as behind the locked doors of your hotel room, you feel too safe.

As we continued to cycle across Belgium, we were still using our trusty printed Google Map and compass routine, stopping at every tourist information centre to ask for general directions or if they had maps of the area. We were following some local advice when we came to a small town and what is possibly the most perfect bakery in the world.

The small village had cobbled streets and a small cemetery in the centre with a plaque to the dead and small graves neatly arranged inside. It was mid-morning and we wanted to purchase a cheap second breakfast, and saw people queuing outside a small bakery with black-fronted windows and a coffee machine outside. The queue looked excited to receive their baked goods as the smell of freshly baked bread rose tantalisingly and beckoned for us to join the eager line. We couldn't resist and joined the back of the queue and salivated over the selection. What followed was the most perfect pain au chocolat I have ever eaten: rich buttery pastry with a generous centre of melted rich dark chocolate and more beautiful Belgian chocolate on top of the pastry. For two hungry cyclists, this place was a dream, and it was made even better when we discovered outside the bakery on a small plinth was free coffee and free mini pastries, just as tasty as the bigger version we had just purchased. This was an oasis of food for us, and we drank coffee and ate treats until we couldn't eat any more. I will always remember that pain au chocolat as something so unexpected and unplanned, a real travel treat. Finding things like this on the road was the reason we travelled by bicycle. If we were in a car or a bus, we would have skipped past this delightful small village and would have missed the chance to sample a real local speciality. I could not tell you now where to find that bakery as we had no idea where we were, but the food memory will live on for a long time.

As we continued south-east, we entered into an area called the Ardennes, which is where it feels like all the hills of Belgium are located and which hosts a professional cycling race called the Tour de Flanders. We popped into the tourist information, and they showed us the maps of the region. Since this is a famous cycling area, all the hills had the gradients marked: 15%, 18%, 22%. Worried, we looked back at our bikes through the window, weighing 35kg and packed full. The road so far had been generally flat, and we were not ready to slog and push up the steep cobbled climbs of the Ardennes. We told the lady behind the counter that we were headed to Istanbul and asked if we could get through Belgium without going over the hills; she kindly took out her local map and marked the way for us to go around the steeper sections. We purchased the map with her routing on, and she also explained to us how the Belgian cycle routes work. First, you find the trails you want to use and write down all the little numbers in your notebook. Then you follow the corresponding number until you reach a turn or intersection and then you simply follow the next number on the list. This was helpful as it meant we were able to use the bicycle paths which zigzagged across farmland and along the Schelde River, and avoid all the problematic inclines.

The final days in Belgium went by quickly, and we followed the small tracks across the country before arriving at the border with The Netherlands. It was a fun final few days as we headed east avoiding the major roads and being able to camp easily in the woodlands or tucked away on farmers fields. On arrival in The Netherlands, we had a quick border crossing beer in Maastricht before cycling over the border again and reaching Aachen in Germany, where we had arranged to stay with Finola's cousin, Nicole. Aachen is a charming German town famous for a large and beautiful cathedral in its centre which was the seat of power for Charlemagne back in AD790. We stayed here for two days chatting with Nicole and exploring the town. It was here we were told, for the first time, that we were able to use our phone as a GPS device and could download maps to use offline.

"You've come from England, following a compass?" Nicole said "Let me show you how to use your phones!" I was amazed. The whole of Europe opened up to us, divided into small files which we could download and plot a route on, or at the very least, a little blue arrow could tell us where we were and if we were heading in the right direction.

With our new GPS, a lot of our navigation problems were solved. I not was aware at the time how much being lost annoyed and frustrated me. In our efforts to leave I had overlooked the simple act of navigation, and by doing this I had caused myself a lot of stress and put a strain on our relationship. Although it was nobody's fault, and being lost was also meant to be part of the fun, I couldn't avoid getting angry when we didn't know where we were. It felt like we were not moving forward and therefore wasting energy.

I was still processing the fact that we had left everything behind on a huge adventure, and by not speaking about it, I used the navigation problems as a way to mask my feelings. Stress is something I found hard to deal with in the beginning, and I tried to counteract it by cycling all the time. Cycling is a great healer, but emotionally I was not working through the two things which were most important at the time: firstly that I was undertaking a massive physical and mental challenge and secondly that being in close confines with Finola was taking its toll on both of us.

I think it is important to note that cycling as a couple is difficult. Although Instagram and blog updates might make it look like the ideal life for two romantically linked travellers, the real story is that when you are cycling all day, every day, when you are tired, dirty and hungry, it can cause you to clash. It is not like everyday life where you have separate friends and careers and other activities to take you away from each other and fill in the gaps. Cycle touring as a couple means that you must be pretty much together at all times and are always making decisions which affect your adventure together. Navigation is a big responsibility. If one person takes over being in charge of the decision-making on your routes and maps, this can lead to arguments, as can other smaller, seemingly incidental things, like who primarily cycles at the front. It may not seem to be a big deal, but if you have one member of the team who is naturally stronger and therefore always sits at the front, it can make the weaker rider feel frustrated and disheartened. We also often clashed about purchasing decisions, camping spots and how long to stop for.

Cycling makes you tired and hungry, and when there is no-one else to blame, it's easy to take your frustration and stress out on the other person. I think the act of cycling together makes it very hard for two people to last together on a long trip, even in platonic partnerships. Very few of the couples I met on the road are still together. As two people who liked to drink and party, this was a massive lifestyle change for us, and since there was no income coming in, this trip was not a two-year holiday. We had to make hard decisions, especially when we rolled into a picture-perfect village during the beginning of summer and the only thing we wanted to do was take a break, buy some lunch and relax. We were both adjusting to this new life and we never gave ourselves any time to adapt, we just hopped right into it from day one. There was also an underlying pressure to go fast enough so the money lasted, though this came more from me than Finola. But while we did argue quite a lot in Europe, the lows were outweighed by the good times rolling through the beautiful countryside and meeting interesting people.

Following Germany, we toured east across Europe, crossing the Czech Republic, Slovakia, and the flat plains of Hungary before reaching Romania after 2.5 months on the road. We were getting fitter, and Western Europe had been the best way to start out bicycle touring as it was relatively flat and easy riding. We understood the cultures and were able to speak English to the people we met. As we travelled east, the differences became more significant, and it was with much excitement that we entered Romania. As we crossed the border, it was the first time our passports were checked, and the first thing we encountered as we cycled out of the border post towards the first big town of Arad was a local farmer crossing the road with about 200 sheep. We stopped and laughed as the road was blocked, while a stressed looking shepherd carrying a crooked cane chased the animals across the road.

As we cycled towards Arad, the number of vehicles picked up, as did the number of horse-drawn carts. Local Romanians today still use horse-drawn carts as a means of getting around and also to sell their local produce. It was with great delight that we saw so many of these traditional vehicles as we cycled into the town.

I felt a sense of wonder but also a slight sense of intimidation, partly due to the impression I had picked up from stereotypes in the British media, and partly because this was the first place we had entered without knowing anything about it in advance. I did not want to get my phone out in public in case someone tried to steal it. This sense of paranoia was a real negative, but I quickly found my perspective changed. I have now realised that it is only by actually going to places which are so-called 'dangerous' that we realise they are often not nearly as dangerous to visit as we are led to believe.

In three years of cycling around the world, I was never mugged or attacked and no-one ever threatened me. It surprises people when I tell them I had a great time in countries like Uzbekistan or Colombia or Honduras, but I truly believe the majority of people out there are not looking to hurt or attack you. In fact, the only time I had things stolen were when opportunistic thieves stole items from the bike when I had left it unattended.

This happened three times. Once in Kazakhstan, when some children stole an mp3 player while I was sleeping in my tent, but then it was my fault to leave it accessible on my bike. The second time was in Thailand when I had left the bike to go and scout a potential camp spot, and as I turned to return to the bike I saw someone going through my front pannier. I shouted, he ran, and I ran as fast as I could to catch him, but he was too fast and ran into a woodland where I was not willing to follow him. I came back to the bike to find that he had stolen a power bank and a small Nokia phone: nothing of real value. The final time was in Chile when the bike was locked up while I was in a super-market toilet. I returned to find my left front pannier open, and everything was missing. I was so angry: my stove was in that pannier and would be hard to replace. I kicked a wall and paced up and down the road before logic kicked in. Maybe the thief had dumped the rest of the contents of the pannier, waterproof trousers, the jacket, the inner tubes. I walked all around the area, hoping to get at least something back. I walked down an alleyway under a bridge and found everything dumped in a small pile. Relieved and amazed, I quickly grabbed it all and checked it through. The thief had abandoned everything, including my stove. It obviously did not look worth much in a tatty black bag covered in black ash! I was relieved and laughed to myself at how lucky I was. On this occasion, I had taken my passport out, along with my valuables before going to the toilet, and I am so glad that I did as I would have lost them forever.

As we continued to cycle through Romania, all our preconceptions were getting broken down, and we were constantly surprised by the level of human kindness we saw. In many of the villages, we met people who wanted to share a beer or vodka with us. Although we spoke no Romanian, we would often join them for a drink, which would lead to three or four beers and a wonky ride for the rest of the afternoon. We found that alcohol was a great leveller, and if we sat and drank with someone, it automatically acted as a bridge between cultures.

We once cycled into a pretty Bulgarian coast town and had locked the bikes to take a short walk around the cobbled town centre overlooking the sea. As we were walking back to the bikes, we met a large drunken man with kind eyes and a red nose who wanted us to come back to his house for a drink. He was mumbling and gestured for us to join him, and we were unsure at first and said no, not through fear but because we were unsure if we wanted to stop or to carry on riding. Sometimes the drive to continue is just too much. He persisted, putting an arm around me and almost pushing us into his house, so we were unable to say "No." His house was small and unkempt with peeling wallpaper and stained sofas and we all sat around a small wooden table in the centre of his lounge area. He offered us cigarettes and rakia, a home-made spirit made from fermented peaches, a staple drink of Hungary, Austria and Bulgaria. We poured the alcohol into little shot glasses, saying cheers before each taking a shot. As soon as we had put our glasses down our host refilled them, and we quickly cheered again. We had three shots in quick succession and started to feel quite drunk.

Our host could not speak English but knew some English songs. His favourite artist was Julio Iglesias, and he sang the song 'Spanish Eyes' over and over again. It was so funny, and soon we were walking down the street, singing 'Spanish Eyes' on route to his friend's house, since his friend was able to speak some English and act as a translator for us. As the four of us drank into the evening, we were told that our host was an Olympian Javelin thrower who represented the USSR in the 1974 Summer Olympics in Montreal. He showed us pictures taken from an old newspaper: a younger version of the man in front of us, with big arms throwing a javelin inside a stadium full of people. It is amazing who you meet on the road, and if we had turned down the offer, we would not have found out we were sharing our evening with a Bulgarian Olympian. We continued singing and telling stories late into the night, with his friend acting as translator. That night we went back to his house and slept on the sofa before waking early as our host had to leave for work at five in the morning. We thanked him and shook his big javelin-throwing hands and cycled off with our hearts warm and our heads fuzzy.

I think that people did not expect us to make it this far, to reach Romania and the end of Europe. Each day we would travel a little bit further across the continent, and in doing so get a little bit further from home. I was happy, and I did not want to stop or go back, I was having the time of my life. The amount of freedom and flexibility was something

I had not experienced before and each day I awoke ready to take on the world. Reaching the coast of Romania would be a significant milestone for us, as it would mean that we had cycled across our first continent. We would meet the Black Sea and therefore have crossed Europe from coast to coast.

As we approached the Black Sea, my ears were filled with the sound of seagulls squawking, like bursts of sarcastic laughter, "ha ha ha."

It felt like they were laughing at me. They were saying "You think you can cycle around the world?", "How cocky can you be, how audacious, do you really think you have what it takes?"

It was at this moment that I knew I did, as I could feel my inner self saying back to these seagulls. "I'm gonna make it. I'll show you." I felt resolute in my decision, and it came at a time when I was reflecting on how far I had come and how far I had yet to go, both in terms of distance and personal development. There are often little things which can make you reassess your trip and think about whether you are on the right lines. The journey is as much a mental one as a physical one. After about two weeks, I knew I was physically capable of cycling 100 kilometres each day and therefore could cycle around the world in my own time. But it is the mental battle which can creep up and cause self-doubt to come in. Why am I doing this? Should I go home and get a job like everyone else? Can I deal with not seeing my family, friends and nephews for years. What if I get hurt? A lot of these questions are best answered while you are cycling as you have the time to think about them properly and therefore check if you are still on the right path.

There is an inner resilience required for bicycle touring, and like most long distance travel, this is underpinned by building a routine. Wake up, prepare breakfast and coffee, eat breakfast, take down the tent, cycle, second breakfast, cycle, lunch, cycle, snack, cycle, camp, dinner, read, sleep. The life of a bicycle traveller is pretty simple when boiled down to these simple tasks. Human life thrives on routine even when on a big adventure. This gives you the platform to be able to go to new places and see new things. Breaking each day up into shorter sections also helps to make the long-term ambition of the adventure manageable. It gives you time to embrace the new cultures and different sights and sounds. Every day you have the ability to eat something new or meet someone for the first time. This is exciting, and for me, it is the structure of this routine which keeps the experience grounded and not overwhelming.

If I had ever stopped enjoying this way of life, I told myself I would simply return home with nothing lost. I would often check in mentally to ensure I was still doing this for the right reasons. I believe that if you do not enjoy something, it is better to stop than to carry on regardless, but if every day you are having more fun than not, then you should carry on. The mental anguish of going on a big journey is something that we may all wrestle with, but you have to live your most authentic life, one which makes you genuinely content. So when the seagulls were mocking me and I asked myself "will I finish this?", my soul sang "yes," and I knew I was on the right path.

*Chapter Six*

# DECISIONS

Getting to the coast also meant we needed to think about visas for the first time since the start of the trip, as we were officially leaving Europe. We were able to purchase our Turkish visas at the border as we were due to cross the border that afternoon. I was ahead of Finola when I noticed a car by the side of the road, with its bonnet up. They were clearly having trouble so I stopped to ask if everything was OK. I helped them for a while, without ever getting to the root of the problem and wished them luck as I waited for Finola to come past. I waited maybe ten minutes more before I started to feel anxious about where she was, worried something terrible had happened. I decided to cycle back to the last place I saw her. If she was not there, it must mean she was ahead, and as I was the stronger cyclist, I would be able to catch her up. Also, as we were to cross the border into Turkey that afternoon, and I had both of our passports, I knew if she was ahead, she would not get too far! I went back, and there was no sign of her, so I turned around and rushed forward to catch up. By now, she must have been 30–40 minutes ahead of me. I knew she would also be worried, so I cycled as fast as I could on my heavy bike. My heart was beating fast due to the quick pace and knowing she would be anxious and worried up ahead.

As you get close to the border, there are many checkpoints, so when Finola had reached the first one, she had asked the local guards if I had gone past. As they said they had not seen me, she was worried that perhaps I had been kidnapped or crashed somewhere. She sat with the guards at the checkpoint for around 20 minutes before I came along and as I did, I saw her jumping up and down and looking very upset. "Where have you been?" She shouted as I tried to explain myself. She had not seen me stop to help out the locals with their car and had cycled straight past.

This happened to us about three times on the trip and was always concerning and stressful. Each time, the situation could have been avoided by putting in place measures to deal with it in advance, such as better communication tools (we only had one phone between us) or a policy of always riding in sight of each other. When we were reunited at the checkpoint, Finola told me she thought I had crossed into Turkey without her, which made me laugh as I knew she could not get into another country without her passport. But stress and anxiety can put strains on your usual way of thinking. After that day, we each carried our own passports.

Entering Turkey was exciting and culturally different from Europe. We crossed the border which lies on top of a 700-meter hill, and then freewheeled downhill all the way to the first town where we stopped for Turkish coffee. We arrived in a dusty town square where the men were all dressed in trousers and shirts with flat caps on and were sitting in the shade to escape the heat of the sun. We were the only white people in the busy town square. The locals all waved and said hello and we waved back although we could speak no Turkish so could only engage in simple communication with them. The Turkish coffee we ordered was made with ground coffee beans mixed with boiling water and therefore was both very strong and very messy.

We sat on large white wooden chairs with big smiles on our faces in this new world. It was about midday, and the bright sunshine bounced off the white walls around us. There was a feeling of organised chaos to the square, people talking and laughing, a donkey roaming, a man pushing a cart full of shoes. It was beautiful and exciting as I felt the thrill of being somewhere totally new, watching and observing life that was so different yet also much the same. As we went to pay for our coffee, the man behind the till told us not to worry and that it had already been taken care of. Welcome to Turkey.

Turkey is famous for hospitality, and I think this comes from their religion, Islam. Muslims are encouraged to receive their guests as visitors from God, so everywhere we went, we were invited to sit, chat, and share a tea. The younger generations generally spoke excellent English, but we got by with hand signals when needed and lots of laughing. As we were riding towards Istanbul, we passed through a small village and as we cycled by, an old man sitting with his friends shouted the word "Chai!" to us. 'Chai' is Turkish for tea and is served black with sugar, in a small glass cup similar to a large shot glass. As we approached, we initially didn't want to stop as we had sat with another family just half an hour ago, but as we got close, the old man got more animated and started to shout "Chai, Chai, Chai Chai, Chai!" while waving his hands up and down. We laughed: how could you not stop when an old man is jumping up and down and waving you over? It is this kind of hospitality that meant we soon grew to love Turkey, and it was great to share a little piece of our adventure with the local people.

We cycled into Istanbul and braced ourselves for the heavy on-rushing traffic and beeping horns that we had been told about, but to be honest, it was actually relatively easy to navigate into the centre on the smaller roads. By following the published bike routes coming in from the west side, we were even able to find a cycle path along the sea which took us into the centre, and while there was some traffic around the old quarter, it was nothing like we feared. In comparison, cities like Hanoi or La Paz are much more challenging to navigate into by bike. Reaching Istanbul meant we had reached the official end of the European Continent. After spending a few days taking in the sights of the old quarter, including the grand bazaar and the blue mosque, we crossed the Bosporus to Fenerbahce, the wealthier eastern side of the city and pushed our bikes onto the Asian Continent for the first time. It was a milestone which needed marking with a beer so that evening we sat on the harbour drinking a few beers and met some locals who we joined for an impromptu party on the harbour walls until two a.m.

It was a fun evening which included a couple of runs back to the alcohol shop. It is possible to get beer in Turkey, but you have to find the right shop, and it is expensive as it is regulated and taxed heavily. We drank with our new friends before camping in the field across from the sea, too drunk to cycle anywhere. In our forgetful state, we left an Aldi shopping bag hanging from a tree branch which contained our food and cooking equipment and in the morning the park cleaners decided this was a rubbish bag and it was gone before we were even up!

Turkey is a large country, and most people apply online for a three-month visa, but since we purchased ours at the border, we only had one month, so we had to push on. This would also help us reach Central Asia before it got too cold. We headed towards Ankara before going north towards the Black Sea as this would be flatter and therefore slightly faster. The road to the Black Sea was great as we got to cycle some of the big passes including the pass of Kavak which has the most beautiful tea shop at the top where you can take a breather and enjoy a hot glass of sweet tea while overlooking the villages below. The people in Turkey were continually surprising us with their levels of hospitality, and everywhere we went, we were on the receiving end of beautiful, warm friendship. We slept in petrol stations as they were always happy to receive us, as well as in mosques and people's homes. We even once just stopped to ask directions and were asked to wait, before the guy returned five minutes later with a pizza to share as we discussed the best route. As we approached the Black Sea and the port of Samsun, we experienced a return of coastal weather patterns and fierce headwinds. The wind blew off the coast, and we were battered by headwinds and some monumental rainfall. We really didn't expect this, and it shows that although you can plan for the weather, you should never leave your waterproof coat behind.

The road along the coast undulated gently and included a large shoulder for us to ride on, so we happily made our way towards the busy port town of Trabzon, where we ran into three cyclists who were also going in the same direction. They were a Turkish couple called Melih and Zida who were both slim with dark hair and dark eyes and their friend Burak who stood out as he had big curly hair to match his outgoing personality. They too, were aiming to cycle around the world, and it was their intention to be the first Turkish couple to do so. Over a cup of tea, our group of two became a group of five as we decided to cycle east together. It was great to travel in a small group, and it took the pressure off Finola and me to keep each other entertained as we had other people to speak to.

Travelling as a group means you can exchange ideas, share the navigation and help each other out. With our new friends being Turkish, they took the majority share of the conversations with the people we met and in the process my Turkish language skills improved by having people around who could translate for me. I enjoyed riding with this new group, and they helped us understand more about Turkish traditions and culture. They were also similar to us in both terms of budget and speed which are two factors that make a difference when riding in a group, as you do not want to hold someone back or be cycling too fast for them yourself. Also, if new friends want to eat at restaurants and stay in hotels and you cannot afford to, it can make for uncomfortable riding as you have to live within your means.

Melih, Zida and Buruk were great to ride with, and we rode from Trabzon together heading east. We stopped with a friend of Melih who owned a hazelnut farm on a hill, and we spent two days exploring some of the mountains and eating hazelnuts picked right from the tree. We swam in the Black Sea on our lunch breaks and shared beers in roadside cafes as we ventured towards Georgia.

It was pretty easy and fun riding as we reached the border between Turkey and Georgia. As we pulled up to the border, I was surprised to see a different script written on the notice boards. I knew nothing about Georgia before we arrived and it turns out they not only have their own language but their own alphabet as well. We all crossed the border excitedly and entered one of the most memorable and fun countries of the entire trip. Georgia proudly declares itself as the country where wine was invented, and it has some of the best organic wine I have ever tasted. It is a rural country outside of the capital, and people all grow their own food and make their own wine, with families sometimes having more than 100 litres of home-made wine in their cellar. The people are also exceedingly friendly. The men are as big as houses with Olympic wrestling being their primary sport. The country also sits just below the Caucasus Mountains, which is one of the most beautiful mountain ranges I have ever seen, with peaks over 5000 meters looking down at you as you cycle harmlessly between them.

We crossed the border with our new friends and obtained our free entry stamp which was nothing more than a formality, before cycling 10 kilometres into Batumi. Batumi is like a little Las Vegas with casinos and bars everywhere. We stopped for a border crossing beer and went for a swim in the warm and salty Black Sea before cycling into the busy town. One of our first aims here was to obtain a visa for Azerbaijan, as we had heard it was easier here than in the capital, Tbilisi, so we decided to stay for a few days.

The first night we camped in the middle of a large field in the centre of the city. Usually, we would never camp out in the open, but we were all feeling a little lazy, so we found a nice secluded spot under a tree, and all five of us rolled out our mats and slept in the warm summer air. We slept until we were all awakened at one in the morning by a stern security guard telling us to move on. We were all fast asleep at this point and were not causing any trouble, but the grumpy policeman would not back down, so we packed up and moved into another area of the park. We gained a few more hours' sleep here until the police came along and told us again to move. We were pretty annoyed so asked him where we could stay, and he pointed us in the direction of an abandoned field around the back of town in which travellers could stay in for free. Happy to have found somewhere, but tired and sluggish we all packed up and moved into our new home. What a great idea to earmark some land for the use of travellers to camp in! We moved in there for three days while we waited for our visas to be ready. Often we would be joined by other travellers, and they either arrived here by word of mouth or were pointed in this direction by policemen. From talking to the other people here, we found out that we were able to obtain free meals and drinks just by gambling a little bit of money in the casinos. In the evening, we would go and play the penny slots in exchange for a buffet dinner and a couple of beers. I think we only spent about two dollars each. Batumi was a fun city, but after three days our visas were ready, and we went back to the office to pick them up. Being British we had to pay $100 each for our visas whereas our Turkish friends got theirs for free. This is due to many visa prices being reciprocal to what one country charges and it seemed that it was quite expensive for the citizens of Azerbaijan to enter Britain.

Once we had our visas, it was time to cycle out of Batumi and see more of Georgia, so we headed north before picking up the road east towards Samitreada and Kutaisi. The cycling was stunning with high mountains providing a backdrop to old monasteries and churches, and once we were out of Batumi, we cycled through beautiful small villages with cheery faces waving back at us. I was really enjoying it here, and it was incredibly cheap compared with Turkey. A bottle of organic wine cost around two dollars to buy, though most people would happily share some of their vast wine reserves with us. We once popped into a small village shop to buy some eggs for lunch and began preparing them on a small bench outside the shop. The shop owner saw us preparing our food and came out with a bottle of wine to have with our lunch, as every meal in Georgia is accompanied by wine.

Finola and I were taking full advantage of the cheap alcohol, and we would often stop for wine breaks in the villages. Melih, Zida and Burak were not drinking as much as us, and this was creating friction between us. This came to a head one evening when we were drinking with some men in their house who had invited us in after we had asked to pick some sweetcorn from their farm. We were drinking vodka and wine, but Melih was not really enjoying himself and wanted to leave. We wanted to stay and both Melih and I, being quite strong-headed people, had a bit of a disagreement.

He said "last drinks," and I said "no," and had another wine with the host. I thought Melih was being rude, and he thought I was leading us into danger, as the host was quite drunk. Melih made it quite clear that he wanted to leave, and we all went together, although our host seemed quite upset that we left. We didn't talk to each other for the rest of the evening even though we had a beautiful campsite up on a hill overlooking an old monastery.

I think it was at this point that we started to drift apart as a cycling group, as while we shared a love for cycling, we all wanted different things from our own trips. We carried on to Tbilisi together, but I was starting to get annoyed that they would go and have their lunches in Turkish restaurants, whereas I wanted to eat Georgian food. They would just speak Turkish in the restaurants, which was difficult for Finola and me. The last week of cycling together felt quite strained, and we should have split up earlier than we did, but it was hard to decide that in the moment, especially when we were both going at the same pace in the same direction. There was also an unspoken understanding that we would reach Tbilisi together. At the time I didn't know how to tell someone I wanted going to go my own way, and perhaps I needed to be more honest in what I was thinking, but I was still learning about myself and life on the road. I did not want to offend my new friends. It is always better to be open and honest in these situations, as often you will find the other people feel the same. Once we reached Tbilisi, Finola and I wanted to stay in a hotel, and our friends wanted to camp, so we found a natural way to split, but I cannot help thinking we could have handled the situation better.

Tbilisi is a great city to recover from the ups and downs of the Georgian countryside, and we stopped, rested, and ate beautiful Georgian food amongst the crumbling walls and old ruins. It was a rest we both needed, and it was nice to be on our own again. One night we went to the football stadium to watch Tbilisi take on another team in the Georgian premier league. The standard was pretty poor, and we made up two of the hundred or so fans watching the game inside the large stadium. The stadium was the national stadium of Georgia and had a capacity for around 10,000, so there was not much noise, but it only cost two dollars per ticket, and it was nice to watch some football. Leaving Tbilisi, it was just Finola and me, and we cycled 100 kilometres from the capital to the border with Azerbaijan in two days before we were quickly processed by the Azerbaijani officials.

Azerbaijan has two routes to cycle in, the northern route, where the mountains are located, which is, therefore, prettier but slower, or the southern route, which is flatter and faster. Usually, we would choose the more attractive way, but the visa we purchased in Batumi started from the date of issue, not the date of entry, meaning once we entered Azerbaijan we only had two weeks to cover the 500 kilometres from the border to the Caspian Sea. This, combined with us reaching the end of the summer season, meant we had to take the faster route to get to Baku. Once in Baku we still needed to organise a ferry over the Caspian Sea to reach Central Asia before the mountain passes would become impassable and dangerous. The route most cycle tourists take is to head south from Azerbaijan to Iran, but since American, Canadian and British passport holders do not have an embassy stationed in Iran, it meant we could not get a visa and therefore were unable to enter the country. Our alternative route meant we had to take a break from cycling and instead go on a mini-adventure by taking a cargo ferry across the Caspian Sea.

We made rapid progress through Azerbaijan and reached Baku in about eight days, before the search for a cargo ferry began. There is no schedule, so you do not know when it will depart. Also, you cannot purchase a ticket in advance, meaning you have to buy a ticket when the boat comes in, but it is a first come first served system, so it requires a bit of luck. The ticket office will call you when they have a boat and can sell tickets, but you don't want to miss out so you must contact the office twice a day to find out information, as they will sell the ticket to whoever gets there first. Once they have a boat ready, you have to travel across the city to the harbour and purchase your ticket for $100. Then you have to get across to another port about 60 kilometres south of Baku where the boat actually sails from. Since you cannot buy a ticket until the day of departure, it means you then have a mad rush to get down to the terminal before it leaves!

Deciding it would be too rushed to cycle to the port we found a taxi with help from our friend Ruslan from the Green Bici Bicycle Club Baku and squeezed both us and the bikes inside. I sat in the boot as there was no room for me inside the car and we paid the driver $50 to take us to the harbour. We only had about an hour until the official departure time, and I was feeling stressed in the boot, not wanting to miss the boat, but the driver was very calm and told us not to worry. I sat there with my eyes fixed to my watch, my heartbeat matching the speed of the taxi. I was sure the boat would leave before we got there, and my face was fixed with worry. I did not want to have to go through this procedure again. As we approached the main gate, I got out and anxiously showed my passport and ticket to the uniformed man at the entrance. We then mounted our bikes and pedalled as fast as we could to the old cargo ship, unsure if it would let us on. On arrival, the captain greeted us and told us not to rush, as the boat would not be leaving for another five hours!

We lashed our bikes alongside the ship's cargo which included two large train carriages smelling of diesel that were being taken to Kazakhstan, along with lots of assorted boxed cargo and some live chickens. We were shown our rooms which were very clean and had twin single beds along with a shower which did not work. There was a dining area where we would be fed breakfast, lunch and dinner, all after the staff had eaten, and was included in our ticket price. *Like a mini cruise*, I thought. It seemed much better than the online reviews of the boats from travellers who had gone before us, and much better than the standard of accommodation we were used to.

We were joined by an Australian couple and two other English cyclists, and it was fun to be able to tell stories and share ideas from the road on our boat adventure. It was a pleasant crossing with lots of card games over dinner, and we ended the night drinking some kind of home-made spirit one of the British guys had with him. It was almost green in colour and was inside a 500-millilitre plastic water bottle and tasted toxic, more like paint thinner than spirit, and soon we were all very drunk. I could not keep up. I fell asleep around midnight, as Finola kept drinking with one of the guys until around six.

I do not know what happened that night, but my jealous brain kicked into overdrive and combined with the hangover I felt sad, depressed and got the idea in my head that I had been cheated on. Although Finola assured me nothing had happened, I think this is the moment things changed for me. I made the decision that I did not want to be in the relationship any more. I was hurt, unhappy and did not want to talk to her. To make things worse, what was meant to be a 24-hour crossing became a 36-hour crossing as the boat had to wait 12 hours for clearance into the port of Kazakhstan! This gave me time to think about my decision, but the more I thought about it, the angrier I became. I was resolute that I wanted to continue on my own, but we were about to cycle through the barren desert of Kazakhstan with sandstorms and extreme heat and a real lack of supplies. I knew it was not fair to leave someone I'd loved in the middle of nowhere, but we needed to have a serious talk about what we both wanted and where we wanted to go in our lives.

*Chapter Seven*
# STRESS

We arrived in the Kazakh town of Aktau, and all I wanted to do was get drunk. Walking through the city in the still morning air, I ignored the new sights of the city, all looming concrete towers and bronze statues. I wanted to bury my feelings of pain and anger, and the only way I knew how to do that was with alcohol. It was all I could think about as we went to find money and accommodation.

I had $100 leftover from Azerbaijan, and I quickly discovered you cannot exchange Azerbaijani money in Kazakhstan. I visited several banks and money changers, waiting in the queues and getting turned away at each occasion. $100 was a lot of worthless notes to carry around, so I started asking around if anyone knew anywhere that might change it. I was pointed in the direction of a colourful market, full of traders in cotton shoes, standing behind racks of colourful spices, and stalls of meat lingering on display in the heat in the sun. I found the local man I was looking for, wearing a patterned shirt which matched the lines etched in his face. He told me he was from Azerbaijan and would therefore buy the currency off me for a rate which was unsurprisingly very favourable to him. Although I was losing out, it was better than nothing, so I agreed to switch my Azerbaijan money for the colourful notes of Kazakhstan.

As we were walking across the street, we were stopped by a local man in his early fifties, with white hair, who spoke excellent English. We told him we were looking for food and accommodation, and without hesitation, he asked us to join him at his home. His house was in the centre of the city and was a large two-bedroom apartment on the top floor of a secure apartment building. His name was Evgeni, and he told us he was a nuclear de-commissioner, helping take down the Soviet nuclear power plants safely over the last ten years. He was an interesting man who shared with us stories of his work and his family. He cooked us dinner that night, and we went out for a beer with the Australian couple from the boat.

I think there are times when I self-medicate through alcohol, seeing it as the answer to my problems. If I was going through a hard time on this trip, I would often turn to alcohol to avoid dealing with the issue. I was not in a good place in Kazakhstan. I was exhausted from thinking about our relationship and how to continue the trip. I knew I needed to talk to Finola but could not find the words, and so I turned to alcohol to give me some relief. I wanted to continue cycling, but at this stage, I knew I really needed some space, and this was just not possible.

The next part of our trip was a challenging ride through the Mangystau Region which was made up of the barren desert of Western Kazakhstan. Finola and I decided that we would ride for 250 kilometres over five days towards a train station on the border where we could load the bikes and get a train to the border with Uzbekistan. I would have liked to carry on to the overland border, but Finola was understandably quite apprehensive of the hard desert cycling, with its limited options for resupply. I knew I needed to put my feelings to one side for the time being and to show Finola that we could move on, both mentally and physically. I saw this compromise as an olive branch to our strained relationship: perhaps we too could move forward even over rough terrain.

The Kazakh desert was hot and sandy, and the road was made of compacted sand rather than tarmac with no shade or anywhere to hide from the beating sun. The sand would whip across the plains and sting our eyes before the wind changed and came straight at us. While the wind gave us some reprieve from the heat, it made for some tough cycling, as the wind pushed into us, almost forcing us backwards. No matter how fast we pedalled, we could not gather up speed. We had to take it in turns to ride at the front to ensure the lead rider would not get too tired. It was the first time in the trip that we had to make changes to our cycling patterns; we now had to cycle earlier in the day when it was cooler, and rest from around 11–3 when the sun was at its strongest. Our desire to find shade meant we often had to look in the strangest places, and once we even rested in the shadow of the shovel end of a large digger which had been left by the roadside, our sandwiches covered in windswept sand!

The heat was oppressive, a downwards force sapping our energy, taking away any joy from the cycling. We had to ride smart and always think about water supplies. We would take our lunch and shade breaks wherever we could and would each consume about five litres of water every day. One of my favourite Kazakh breaks was close to the town of Beyneu. We were resting in a bus stop, and the heat was taking its toll, so we started to fall asleep. In our dizziness, a small squat man, with short hair and a worried look on his face turned up in a little Fiat insisting we follow him to his house and telling us it was too dangerous to sleep at the bus stop. We wearily woke and followed him to his home on the edge of the village where he introduced himself as Baijan and told us to lie down on some large mats he laid out for us while he would cook us something to eat. We quickly passed out and before waking a few hours later to find Baijan had made us some meat soup and salad.

Corba, a meat soup, is one of the staple dishes in Central Asia and consists of a tasty stock with a chunk of beef or lamb on the bone. We all sat and ate together and shared tea while Google translated his Russian into our English. He told us about his family and took us to see their farm on the other side of the village. It was a real cultural exchange, with Baijan asking lots of questions about England. He showed us his horses and camels and his favourite t-shirt, with a picture of Vladimir Putin holding a shotgun and machine gun! It was an honour to share our time with him. It was a great introduction to desert life, and we slept in his house that night. In the morning we had a classic Kazakh breakfast of bread, cheese and camel milk before saying our goodbyes. Baijan followed us out of the village in his car to make sure we were safe, then he went back to his family, and we went back into our sandstorm.

Cycling past Beyneu towards the train station we passed a sign which in both English and Russian simply states "Welcome to the dangerous section." We paused for photos, hoping it just meant fewer supplies and shops there, as opposed to the region being filled with bandits trying to rob us. We cycled past smallholdings selling fermented yak milk which was drunk by the passing Kazakh men. This slightly salty and alcoholic drink is pretty disgusting on first taste but does have quite a kick if you are looking for something to keep you awake while driving along the long straight roads. Perhaps this was why they called it the dangerous section. The broad, flat landscape made for some epic photos, but the cycling was actually relatively mundane, with the wind against us and nothing to see, while being forced to stop for long periods to avoid the midday heat.

After five days, we arrived at the train station, hot, sunburnt and tired. The smell of diesel overpowered us as we approached the compact ticket office. It was not expensive, and they did not charge extra for the bikes. We would, however, have to change trains at the border as the two countries had different train companies. The bikes would be offloaded from one train ready for us to load onto the next one. This felt like a little adventure itself and a welcome break from cycling, and was also a chance to rest on the narrow bunks in our train carriage. We caused quite a stir with the other travellers in our four-bed cabin since it was the first time they had seen western travellers on the same train as them.

At the changeover, we had to present our passports and show all of our stuff to the immigration police. They were very thorough, as Uzbekistan is a highly controlled state and if you are found with anything contraband, including things like certain computer games, pornography or codeine, it can lead to a small amount of jail time. They made us take everything out of the bags so they could check before they went through our medicines with a fine-tooth comb, but with nothing illegal, they let us continue on our way. Uzbekistan is not only strict with arrivals and customs but also with its own politics. When we were there the current President, Islam Karimov, was entering his third re-election with over 90% of the vote. Uzbekistan was also the country with the second highest rate of modern slavery with 3.97% according to the Walk Free Foundation and also requires its citizens to apply for exit visas if they intend to leave.

Passing through the second train were money changers and locals selling lots of home-cooked food and goods. We bought some local dumpling soup which was delicious and changed our leftover money for Uzbek Som. Uzbek money is controlled just like the rest of the country, but high inflation and the fact they only have two denominations of bills means that for $100 worth of Kazakh money I received nearly a million Uzbek Som. Since there were only denominations of 1000 or 5000, I ended up with a stack of money about six inches thick. The lady counted it with the ease of a magician, the notes moving quickly through her hands. There was no way I was going to be able to count it without spilling it all over the train carriage, but one of the other passengers helped me count it to check it was right. Everyone in Uzbekistan carries around a tote bag or rucksack to put their money in. It is a crazy situation, and with the demand and higher rate for dollars on the black market, you can often be walking around with stacks of notes 12 inches tall for about $150 changed. The local people are accustomed to this and can count it quickly and efficiently, which is always impressive, but when I counted out the money, it was a tedious and time-consuming affair.

Our train pulled into the town of Nukus, our first port of call in Uzbekistan, a country famous for the beautiful and dazzling architecture and landscapes of the Silk Road. Nukus was however an outlier in architecture. The dusty, sand covered buildings huddled together around a dirty train station made for a disappointing first view of this new country. We were tired and wanted a room to recharge ourselves and our electronics, so we went looking for a hostel or cheap hotel in the little town. We asked around but could not find anything, so we asked in a little shop across the road where we bought some water. Unbelievably the young woman running the shop spoke English and said we could stay with her. This Central Asian hospitality was so impressive: we were being treated to food and a place to sleep by complete strangers wherever we went. You would not find this attitude in Western Europe, and it is only when you go out to see for yourself the places that some people call dangerous, that you realise they are full of wonderful, kind people.

We had a great time staying with our host, and her mother even slaughtered one of the family chickens for our dinner. This was a great occasion and something we were honoured to be a part of. We ate home-made bread and chicken and shared some vodka. The following day we took photos of the family and said our goodbyes as we headed for the first Silk Road town on the route which was Khiva. The Silk Road of Uzbekistan comprises three famous old cities, Khiva, Bukhara and Samarkand, and is essentially just one main road which connects these cities. Khiva is perhaps the oldest and in my opinion the most beautiful as it has kept its original charm behind the crumbling old walls which surround the city. The walls are yellow and brown, made with a mix of clay and straw. It is a low city with no high rise buildings, as nothing could be built higher than the pillar of a minaret in the centre of town.

We each explored this city on our own as we did not want to spend the day together. It was a shame, but I needed the time to think, and I did this mainly in a small bar across from the hotel. I was dealing with everything pretty badly at this point, and the only way I could find contentment in my life at this point was by cycling or drinking. We only spent one day in Khiva as I wanted to keep moving. Looking back, I was pretty awful to be around during this time. I was dealing with inside turmoil but by not letting anything go, I was just taking everything out on Finola. The lack of trust was horrible, but without communication, nothing could be resolved, and the ill feelings lurked under the surface. The alcoholic side of me was coming back, and I was drinking too much. The tour was becoming more about getting through the day than seeing what was around the next corner. We needed to change the dynamic, but without talking things through, nothing was going to change. We tried talking in Khiva, but I was too drunk, and it quickly became an argument. We both agreed to try to move on and continue, but knew it was going to be tough. We were in an area of incredible natural beauty, but here I was struggling to take it in.

The following day we cycled towards Bukhara, the second city on the Silk Road, about a five-day cycle ride through the desert. The road to Bukhara was pretty flat, and it was hot cycling through the desert, but the camping was amazing. Most nights, we would camp out in the desert staring at the millions of stars and awaken to find small golden scorpions hiding under our bags. They never seemed to come near the tent, and we made sure we put our shoes inside the tent overnight for safety. Each morning they would look back at us when we moved our bulky panniers, each of us unsure if one was going to try and hurt the other before quickly running away to another hiding place in the desert.

For the first time on the trip, I began to find the food to be a problem. I believe this is quite common in Uzbekistan where you can buy small roadside pastries called somsa which are similar to a samosa but filled with meat and fat and cooked inside a clay oven. Warm, highly calorific and tasty, but as we approached Bukhara, I had a bad case of food poisoning. I should have stopped and rested, but I wanted to get to the city so we could stay in a hostel and I could fully recover. Finola rode ahead, with me behind. I was feeling unwell and was cycling slowly whilst also standing up. My stomach was gurgling, and I knew I was in trouble as I went over a small pothole.

My face contorted. There was nothing I could do as I felt my stomach go and my bowels released themselves as I went over the little bump. Horrified, I quickly stopped on the side of the road to review the mess before running into some long grass to clean myself up. Luckily when you are cycle touring, you always have a change of boxers with you! I quickly changed and buried my dirty boxers in the long grass. When you are on the road, you have no option but to carry on, so although I felt unwell and worried that this might happen again, I had no choice but to ride slowly onwards towards the town. Thankfully, we arrived in the city later that day. We found a cheap but charming room and had a quick look around town before I had to go back to the hotel and spend the night jumping between the bathroom and bed. This was my first real sickness of the tour, and I was lucky to be inside not stuck in a tent in the desert. I felt pretty rotten, but knew it was important to rest.

I decided I would not eat any more somsa here in Central Asia, which was a shame as they were very cheap and delicious, but I couldn't risk it again.

Bukhara is beautiful, with a large minaret decorated in colourful blue and white mosaics towering over the city. We stayed in the city for three days before my stomach had cleared up, and I felt good enough to be back on the road, fit and healthy again.

It had been good to relax for a bit in Bukhara, and although I spent most of the time in the hotel room, it was what I had needed: sometimes you just need a rest and to be out of the elements for a few days. The next city on the Silk Road is Samarkand, and it is the jewel of Uzbekistan. Samarkand is famous for the large Rajasthan which sits in the middle of town. It was a comfortable 250 kilometre ride from Bukhara, and we reached the famous city in just two and a half days. It was really special to explore the Rajasthan, and it was even better when we found a small side entrance which we were able to sneak into, avoiding paying $10 to enter. It is a special place and quite stunning to look at from a distance, but it is ruined by the huge amount of useless tat for sale inside. You can buy all shapes and sizes of mosque statues, handbags and scarves, and this commercialisation spoiled the experience for me. There are also large numbers of tourists who flock here on tour buses, so it feels a lot less authentic than the cities of Khiva or Bukhara. It is however absolutely stunning, and an architectural marvel, as are the graveyard walks around the city. Beautiful blue and white mosaic tiles line the walls, making it seem so distant from the red brick back home. While beautiful to look at, I was not enjoying my time in Uzbekistan. I tried to like it, as I had been so excited before I had left, but I found the distances between towns, the deserts and bureaucracy really tough. That, in addition to getting ill, and Finola and me not getting along, made it a tough country for me to be in and it is somewhere I would not go back to in a hurry.

We made the decision to head straight to Bishkek, the Capital of Kyrgyzstan, rather than going via the Fergana Valley towards Osh. We would head into Kazakhstan once more through Tashkent, the capital of Uzbekistan, and into the city of Shymkent, rather than taking the tougher, longer route through the Pamir Mountains. We would then drop down into Kyrgyzstan and into the Capital, Bishkek, where we would collect our Chinese visas before cycling over the highest and coldest mountains of the whole trip so far. It was good for me to be back in Kazakhstan, and we celebrated with a border crossing beer in a little restaurant just over the border. Finola and I finally spoke about our relationship, what we both wanted and how we were feeling. We agreed to carry on together and to try to get on better. We both knew we had some hard cycling ahead of us, and neither of us wanted to face that alone. It was the right choice as I was as unsure of the cold climes as she was, and we needed to cycle the mountains together for support and safety. The relationship was on the rocks, but the trip was carrying us through as it had done from the beginning. Cycle touring was the last thread holding us together.

## Chapter Eight

# THE COLD

Bishkek is a Soviet-era concrete capital with grey buildings everywhere, but poking their heads up over the drab grey towers are the beautiful mountains of the Pamirs and lower Himalayas. It was amazing to walk around the small side streets, where you frequently find yourself pausing to gaze up at the mountains above you. Looking up at these giants, I felt a pull, as if the mountains were asking me to take on the challenge, and like any challenge, I knew it was not going to be easy but would be rewarding at the end.

We had contacted our accommodation in advance, choosing to stay at the famous AT House in the city centre. The AT House is a community house for bicycle travellers set up by its hosts, Angie and Nathan. We arrived through the wooden doors and were immediately greeted by a rabble of road-weary bicycle tourists who made us feel very welcome straight away. There were 12 other cyclists staying at the house. We all bonded as we sat around the outside table, sharing stories, working on blogs, and discussing plans for the future. Finola and I spent 12 days in total in

Bishkek; this was the longest stop for a long while and something we both needed. We stayed so long for two reasons: firstly we were waiting for a package from my father with some cold-weather gear inside to help us with the temperatures on the high passes; and secondly, we had to apply for our Chinese visa which was a complicated, slow, and expensive process.

The best way to get a Chinese visa in Bishkek is to go through an agency who will help with the process, acting as a middle-man for the language and cultural barrier. It is expensive, but they promise you a visa in seven days for $150, and they deal with the interview process and forms, both of which are in Chinese. You have to make a fake itinerary which suggests you will fly to a popular Chinese city and look at the regular tourist sites. This is because the authorities do not want tourists in the west, since this is where a lot of the Uyghur Chinese people live. These people are Muslim rather than Buddhist and are culturally more linked to Central Asia rather than China. The Chinese government has actively tried to reduce the number of Muslims in this area with the mass immigration of Han Chinese people, pushing the Muslim population out and placing large numbers into internment camps dressed up as re-education centres. At the time of writing, "at least 1 million Uyghurs have been interned since 2017 in more than 85 identified camps within Xinjiang" reports PBS News.

To complete the visa application process, you have to attend an interview where they test you on your travel plans, so you must learn your fake itinerary off by heart and never mention your bicycle. Through our translator from the visa agency, they asked me questions like where I would be on a certain date, and I had to make sure I gave the correct city. This was quite nerve-racking, but both Finola and I passed the interview, and then we had another five-day wait while the visas were processed.

In the meantime, we waited for the package from England. My dad had written the correct address, but he put the wrong country at the end of the address and so the package was sent back home! We had all our essential winter gear in the package including base layers, gloves and pogies for the handlebars, so we couldn't leave without it. I had many Skype chats with my dad and DHL to arrange for the parcel to be redelivered. It was only on the day before we were due to leave that it finally arrived, and we were so happy and relieved as it would mean that cycling in the cold temperatures would be much safer. The package also unexpectedly contained two big bars of Dairy Milk chocolate which went down a treat with our travelling friends from the hostel. After buying a couple of new winter sleeping bags in a sports store in Bishkek, we were ready to take on the mountains. On the day we were due to leave, Nathan told us he did not want us to pay for our accommodation. A lovely gesture from a guy who opened up his whole house to passing strangers each summer, a real road angel who made this little hostel a warm and welcoming place in the middle of the concrete city.

The weather was getting colder, and it was towards the end of October when we left, with temperatures as low as -15 being reported over the high passes. We left feeling a little worried, but with the confidence of the ignorant, we cycled out of Bishkek and into the snow.

The day we left, the weather changed, and it started snowing down upon us. Having never cycled in the snow before, it was not long before we were wet and cold through as the settled snow melted over our warm gloves and shoes. We had to stop regularly in local restaurants for coffee and a chance to warm up, meaning we only made around 60 kilometres that day, before camping behind an old shed by the road.

The snowfall continued overnight, and in the morning everything was frozen solid: our tent, our bikes, and our chains. Everything. We needed to heat water to pour on our bike chains to get them moving again. We had to massage our tent poles to free the ice from inside them using our only pairs of gloves to get them folded and back in their bag. Since they were now soaking wet, we could not put them back on so had to cycle that morning with no gloves in the freezing cold air. Socks helped out a bit, shouting helped more! We quickly backtracked and rode to the nearest shop to buy extra food, water and gloves. Riding with no gloves, or even worse, wet gloves, is awful and is something that happened much too frequently for my liking, as I was continually losing or misplacing my gloves as I dealt with packing the gear each morning. With the cold taking little bites out of our spirits, the mountain views would quickly remind us why we were riding here, giving us the lift we needed. As we climbed, we would be rewarded with a new peak or flowing stream to look at, and it was a real pleasure to cycle through this ever changing landscape.

The gradient required slow and steady cycling, but as soon as we reached the plateau, we were surrounded by mountains over 6000 meters high looking down on us. The first night up the mountain we climbed to over 2000 meters and with the temperatures around -12 we were absolutely freezing, even though I was using two sleeping bags! I zipped both bags up, so the only exposed skin was my mouth blowing out cold air, as I restlessly stirred to keep warm throughout the night. We vowed to never camp above 2000 meters again, as it was just too late in the season, so from then on we sought guest houses or small hostels to stay in. The cold would sap our phone battery, meaning we had no way to know how far the next hostel might be, so when we saw some smoke billowing out of a small house, we often knocked on the door for a cup of tea and a chance to warm up against the wood burner and ask directions.

Most small houses here are lived in by poor mountain folk, so they are more than happy to sell you a cup of tea and sit and talk with you for a while as you warm up. One time we called into such a tea house and were greeted by a small Kyrgyz man in his early twenties wearing winter clothes and a colourful woollen hat. We asked for tea, but he had only one tea bag to share among the three of us. We were happy to talk to him and drink tea, and he also gave us each a frozen apple to eat, telling us apples will not go off once frozen, though you had to let it thaw first! He was a real gentleman, and we tipped him along with the price of the tea bag since it was just so lovely to be inside. He had a thermometer on the outside of his hut, and he told us it was -7... in the middle of the day!

These types of guest-houses were a saviour to us on the mountains. Each small hotel would welcome us in, and each one was different. Once we stored our bicycles in the meat locker and then were shown to our room before returning downstairs in the morning to a breakfast of five fried eggs and bread each. This was hearty mountain food. One house we stayed in was a family home, and we played with their small daughter and then fell asleep in the lounge after a dinner of lagman, an Asian noodle dish. We awoke that morning to find six people sitting in the house all around the fire. The cold weather really brings people together, and in the freezing climates, you can that everyone looks out for each other. The scenery, like the cold, was breath-taking, and the horizon brought views I had only seen in photographs, with snow-capped peaks silhouetted against a bright blue sky.

The first pass we reached after three days of uphill cycling was called the Ala-Bel Pass at 3125 meters. We triumphantly celebrated with an impromptu snowball fight before cycling downhill for two days. The road down from the pass was a series of sweeping turns, with each one presenting a majestic and breathtaking view. The curves of our smiles matched the beauty of the road as we weaved down the mountain. It was simply the most stunning road I have ever ridden. We descended, as the snow slowly made way for black rock before turning into green and yellow grass. As we reached the gorges and lakes of Jalal-Abad, the sun came out and we were able to strip off into summer weather clothing as we were joined by galloping wild horses and fluttering irridescent butterflies. The pure unadulterated joy of that descent made all the hard effort of getting to the top worth it and even now brings a tear to my eye just thinking about how beautiful that road was.

The second big pass is called the Taldyk Pass and is reached by climbing a winding mountain road up to 3600 meters. The uphill of the Taldyk brought strong winds which either smacked us in the face or gave us a shove forward depending on which direction we were facing as we snaked up the climb. At around 3300 meters Finola stopped and got a lift from a passing van, but as I was so close to the top, I resolutely rode the remaining 300 meters to the summit.

Finola told me to meet her in the town of Sary-Tash, and I continued up the mountain alone. I wanted to overcome this challenge, and I was not to be defeated. I reached the top, happy that I had climbed the mountain alone and proud of myself for doing so. I used to be in the lowest grade for PE at school and had once weighed over 17 stone, but I was now as fit as I had ever been, and my body was working in perfect harmony with my mind and my bike. I posed for a few quick photos, before jumping on my bike and going back downhill towards Sary-Tash. The only downside of the descent was that the sun had melted all the snow on the top and the water had runoff in my direction, freezing to ice on the road back towards town. I fell twice trying to manoeuvre the bike safely down the sharp decline, once in front of a group of bemused road workers who all stopped working as I fell right in front of them. I quickly got up and rode away, embarrassed.

I reached the town of Sary-Tash, which really is just a tiny mountain village at a crossroad between Kyrgyzstan and China. I spotted Finola, and she showed me to a small hostel with lots of blankets and radiators where we ate spaghetti and warmed up. It was around -20 that night, and I was tucked inside four duvets to keep warm. After breakfast, which was again spaghetti, we left to head towards the Chinese border, about 60 kilometres away. We needed to reach the border that day, as with no towns on the way we did not want to camp out in the extreme cold. When the sun was up, the weather was not too much of an issue, but at night it became much too cold to camp outside. We had ridden about 10 kilometres in around 45 minutes and became worried that we might not reach the border in daylight so we decided to stop and see if we could hitch a ride in a passing truck. After waiting about 40 minutes, becoming increasingly anxious that this was time wasted and not time gained, a large red truck passed and offered us a ride. We threw our bikes in the back of the empty lorry and climbed into the cab. The driver dropped us off just before the border, and we thanked him. He did not want any payment, which was lucky as we only had about £5 of local currency left. We had made it to the border, and we were both excited to see what China would bring. It was so far away in both distance and cultural identity from where we had ever been that it was a genuinely memorable border crossing. We were also happy to have made it over the highest passes of the trip so far and survived our coldest winter.

The mountains were the most significant challenge we had faced on this trip so far. We were both tough and hardened to the road by this point, but this was real cold weather stuff, and we had no previous experience in this kind of cycling. There had been a definite degree of anxiety going into Kyrgyzstan, and we knew the only way we were going to get through this beautiful but wild landscape was if we worked together. We had to put our troubles away for a time to overcome the cold and the inherent dangers that came with it. It was not easy but we both rallied and became a team again, a feeling we had not had since the early days in Europe. In overcoming the mountains, we thought we had overcome the issues with our relationship. The wild nature, the cold, the hunger, the lack of information and supplies meant that we were forced to pull together and grew closer as a result. By being in the elements the truth was exposed, like the mountain peak open to the weather all year round. It felt like our protective skins had been shed to reveal a softer core beneath, showing that there was still something there, some kind of bond between us. The mountains gave us hope that we could continue together, that everything was going to be easier from now on. I just hoped we would be able to remember the lessons learnt in the cold.

*Chapter Nine:*

# THE LONG ROAD

We were both excited and happy as we realised how far we had come on our heavily laden bikes, and by just cycling a little bit every day we had now arrived in the far east, albeit the most western point.

The Chinese border is essentially 140 kilometres of barren no man's land. The Chinese authorities insist that to cross the border, you must take a taxi. Unfortunately for us, we did not have enough money on us, so we had to pay extra to ensure the driver would take us through the border and then onto the next town where we could get some cash out.

We laughed nervously, as we realised we could not read or communicate with anyone: even the road signs were in both Chinese and Uyghur, the local dialect which we could not understand at all. Western China was harder than in Central Asia as there were fewer English speakers and even fewer tourists here. The only way we could communicate was by using technology, and we downloaded an app, called

Waygo, which worked offline and would enable us to translate Chinese characters into English. This meant we had some idea at least if we were about to order noodle soup or fish head soup!

Navigating in Western China is pretty easy as there is only one road, the main highway which runs from the border all the way to Lanzhou in the west. The road is called the G314, is 1500 kilometres long and links Kashgar and Lanzhou. Being a new Chinese road, there was a large shoulder for us to ride in and therefore it was pretty safe. The only downside of such a route is that it is monotonous, with cold weather and harsh winds battering us every day. Our food became the staples available in petrol stations – instant noodles, rice crackers and salty biscuits – with the occasional restaurant meal thrown in if we came across one.

When you are cycling on a motorway, it is often impossible to reach the next exit junction by the end of the day. High fences lined the road, keeping the animals off, but also preventing us from camping out in the desert. So the only place to sleep was underneath the road. About every five kilometres there would be a small underpass for either animals or water, and we would duck down into these and set up a camp stealthily underneath. It was quite daunting the first time as lorries would drive over our camp with a loud da-dump, and we'd wonder if our little hideout would collapse, but we quickly got used to this, and it had the added benefit of protecting our camp gear and bikes from the nightly snowfall. We ventured slowly east, going past the town of Turpan. Turpan sits 150 metres below sea level, the second lowest point on the planet, making it the hottest place in China during the summer months, and warm enough to cultivate grapes there, even in the winter. These are turned into raisins rather than wine in this mostly Muslim area.

The road east is relatively uneventful and we were able to cycle an average of around 100 kilometres a day before camping underneath the road. The cycling here was uneventful, flat and repetitive, and our days were spent listening to music and podcasts. After about two weeks of wearisome cycling, we arrived in the township of Hami where we took a $25 a night hotel. Unfortunately, the cheaper hotels do not allow tourists and are only for locals, so we were quickly directed to the poshest hotel in the city where we took its most affordable room! It was a luxury for us, and they had a British movie channel, so we stopped here for two days whilst we rested and ate Chinese food. It was good to rest as the road was tough and the monotony of it all was relentless.

We needed a strict routine as the mornings were so cold we did not want to leave the warmth of our beds, but we had to get on the road to cover the next 100km of unchanging ground for the day. On leaving Hami, we were hit with the famous Hami headwind, which we nicknamed the Hami Hurricane as it was so strong. Winds of sixty kilometres per hour meant that we were only able to cycle at around eight kilometres per hour on the flat! This, along with the ice which had built up on the shoulder, meant it was challenging and dangerous cycling for us. Cold winds weathered our faces which reflected back on the dangerous ice. It was so hard riding and not at all fun. After two relentless days, we had had enough and agreed to stop and try to hitch-hike to the next town. After waiting for 20 minutes, and with us getting colder with each passing gust, we decided we would have to push on with the wind in our faces as we were getting too chilled. We had continued for about half an hour, and I was some way in front of Finola when I saw she had stopped to speak to some road workers in their van. I knew she was asking for a lift but not wanting to stop, I continued, knowing they would come and get me if they agreed to save us from the hurricane. The road workers soon pulled alongside, and four smiling Chinese faces welcomed me to join them. They put my bike into the back of their truck and took us 90 kilometres to the state border where Kashgar Province connects with Gansu Province. Their kindness came at a perfect time, and it was a real relief to fast forward out of this horrendous wind. I would not recommend this road for cycling as it is pretty dull, and the cold and the headwinds make it more of a slog than a bicycle tour, detracting from the excitement of reaching the far east.

The one highlight of cycling along this road was reaching the most western part of the Great Wall of China. This part of the great wall receives fewer tourists than the more popular sections in Beijing, and as a result, when we went climbing the big steps, we were the only people there. We had the freedom to explore without the masses, and it meant we could take in the scale of the project and spend a lot of time imagining we were protecting China from the Mongol hordes.

The Chinese visa we received in Bishkek was for 30 days with the option to extend only once, meaning we would have to cycle a minimum of 150 kilometres each day to cross China in the allotted time. For us this was impossible, so once we had seen the Great Wall in Jiuquan, we put our bikes onto a bus which would take us the 1500 kilometres in just twelve hours rather than another 30 days of boring highway cycling. This meant we could enjoy more of our time in the southern provinces, which also happen to be warmer and more alive compared to the long, dull highways of the north. China is such a vast landmass than you can cycle into a more tropical weather system just by heading south and this was our intention as we travelled away from Lanzhou.

The ride from Lanzhou to Chengdu was slowly getting more tropical as we rode along small village paths and up over small, remote mountains. The villages were beautiful, and often the children would run and cheer us as we cycled past them. Waterfalls cascaded down the road side and cars stopped for an impromptu car wash. The one downside of taking the smaller village roads is that these were usually built before the highway, and since the motorway network is now the de facto method of getting around, the smaller roads have fallen into disrepair. It is more like climbing over cobbles rather than roads. I remember one road which I nicknamed Cobble Mountain. It was a pass of 2700 metres, but the road was made entirely of conjoined cobbles meaning we had to work hard to cycle over this bumpy ground and even harder going back down, holding our brakes to stop us going too fast as we were shaken all over by the cobbles. We would often go past little villages where we were looked upon as aliens, people shocked to see us go past. It was so funny as whenever we went to a shop to pick up some food, people would follow us around the shop taking selfies and looking in our shopping baskets. They wanted to see what the white people would buy, which was lots of noodles and vegetables but very little in the way of chicken feet and unidentified meat!

One of the real highlights of this part of the trip was the Panda Sanctuary in Chengdu. For an entry fee equivalent to six pounds, you can spend the afternoon walking around the enclosure and see pandas from tiny babies to fully grown adults in an environment which is working to save them. It is a beautiful place, and it warms your heart to watch these funny creatures, rolling around and playing in their enclosures.

Heading south out of Chengdu, I was starting to find cycling through China draining due to the considerable differences in culture and language. We had been in China for six weeks at this point and I felt we were not gelling with the local community in the manner in which we had in Central Asia. The roads were challenging, and I was feeling exhausted from the effort we put in to cross the Taklamakan Desert highway and the constant struggle with language. It took a lot of effort, and I needed change: I was road-weary, and after crossing the mountains I think the cold had entered into my bones and I needed to find some warmer weather. So I came up with a plan for us to reach Vietnam for New Year's Day, and in a "the grass is always greener" outlook I made it my mission to see in 2016 somewhere in Vietnam. It was Christmas Eve when we reached the vibrant city of Kunming, a beautiful city with a large lake in its centre with temples and shops mixed together around it. To celebrate our first Christmas on the road we wanted to spend it with other travellers, so we found a simple hostel in the centre which offered a Christmas dinner.

After checking into a double room, we went out and purchased each other Christmas gifts, and did a little food shopping for the big day, before returning to the hostel for a relaxing evening and Christmas meal of spicy barbecue shredded turkey wraps! Turkey, yes, but this was a long way off a traditional English Christmas dinner. The food was lovely, and the company was fun as we shared a couple of beers before retiring to bed. The following day was Christmas, and we woke to open presents and to go for a walk around the lake. It was a pleasant walk, but as we sat under some trees, listening to music from a speaker Finola had bought me, I was not really feeling very well. I had no energy and knew something was wrong. Very soon, the Christmas spirit wanted to leave me from both ends, and I had to retreat to the hostel to rest. It seems that the spicy shredded barbecue turkey had not agreed with me, and I spent that day in bed. Sick again. The sickness only lasted about 24 hours and the following day we left the hostel. After a rubbish Christmas I wanted to ensure we had a fantastic New Year, so welcomed the road south to take us to the border with Vietnam.

We were two days away from the border when we woke one morning by the side of the main highway. We had climbed over the road barrier and camped in some scrubland about 200 metres away. It was a cold morning, and we had started with a quick breakfast before packing everything away. We loaded everything onto the bikes, and then I had the job of lifting them over the barrier to continue on our way. I lifted my bike over and then went back to grab the second bike. As I was stepping over the barrier with the bike in my hand, I landed wrong, and my foot made contact with the ground before rolling my ankle sharply to the right. I dropped the bike and fell instantly to the ground with a scream; something was wrong. I sat on the hard shoulder with cars whizzing past, holding my ankle with a very concerned look on my face. Pain radiated up my leg, but I could at least move it, so I was sure it was not broken. Looking down I saw my ankle had swelled up to the size of a grapefruit almost instantly. I sat on the road cursing my luck as Finola came to see what was wrong. She looked at my ankle, and her face dropped with concern. We were five kilometres from the next town on the side of the main road. We had to either continue or find help. I tried walking, but my ankle hurt too much. Maybe I could sit on the bike and roll, but the road rose slightly on an incline and pedalling hurt too much. We rested for around half an hour, but knew we had to do something so with one arm on my bike and one arm on the railing I pushed myself slowly towards the next town. I was in agony, and had only gone around 100 metres before having to rest again.

We had another five kilometres to go and knew we needed help, so I sat on the barrier, dejected and annoyed while Finola put out her thumb and tried to get me a lift into town. It was not long until a small sedan car pulled into the hard shoulder to see what was wrong. The vehicle contained a young Chinese couple and their mother, and as luck would have it, the young couple could speak a good level of English. Their names were Rennie and Rico, and they agreed to take me to a local hospital they knew in town. I sat in the car whilst Rico, a young man of about 25, took my heavy bike and rode it behind us, before meeting us back in the hospital.

The hospital was a small building with a waiting room, some consulting rooms to the side and the ward beds on the first floor. We were shown in and with our Chinese heroes translating for us, I was looked after straight away. X-rays were taken before my ankle was wrapped in a bandage and a red paste of Chinese herbs and medicines was applied between each layer of the dressing. The paste smelt of rust and I was told this would help me heal. Everyone in the hospital came around to see us. I think we were the first western patients, as even the owner and head doctor came to visit us. The X-rays confirmed I had a bad sprain, and the only remedy was anti-inflammatory painkillers and rest.

I was given some crutches to help me get up the stairs to the ward above. There were just four beds in this ward, and

I was told to rest. Finola was also given her own bed, and I was told I would need to rest here for three days. I guess we could have got a hotel, but we were under the guidance of the hospital staff, and this seemed as good a place as any to rest. The staff, nurses and doctors at the hospital treated us more like guests than patients, and it was not long before Rennie and Rico were back with gifts from the shop including bread and milk to help me recover. The next three days were a dream; we were treated like royalty as we were taken to dinner and breakfast every day by the hospital owner. We were treated to Chinese hot pot each night and traditional noodle soup each morning. The owners even took us on a city tour along with Xi, the man who was in charge of looking after us. It was a beautiful experience to be looked on as guests rather than patients and I recovered quickly. After three days, I no longer needed crutches to get around, I was feeling stronger and told the doctors I would be able to leave the next day.

I was relieved, and my relief turned to joy as that night everyone came to our room, and we had a little party in the hospital ward with pizza and cups of tea. Rennie and Rico were there, and they gave us presents, shampoo which looked like a blood bag and some food for the road. I was overwhelmed with their generosity and kindness: these two passers by had stopped to pick up some weird looking western cyclists, and we had become close friends. The day we were due to leave I walked downstairs and took photos with everyone and thanked them for their time and hospitality. They then presented me with the bill for just

£15, which covered the cost of the X-rays only. It was a real honour to be treated there, and although New Year's Eve was seen from the inside of a hospital ward, I had a much more organic and real experience than just partying somewhere in Vietnam.

I often think of how lucky we were to meet Rennie and Rico and how they really helped me out. This experience dramatically changed my whole opinion of China, and it is moments like this which shape the experience and allow your real opinions to be formed. We were welcomed so honestly from people who only wanted to help, who saw two people struggling, unable to speak, unable to understand. Still, shared human experience overrode all the differences, and they helped us without worry or charge.

It was with a tear in my eye that we cycled away from the hospital, pausing for one last photo and wave before heading off. Ten minutes later I crashed straight into another cyclist coming the other way! Perhaps my spirit wanted to return to the hospital, but the Chinese medicine held firm and my ankle was fine. We continued our journey towards the temperate delights of Vietnam, just two days ride away. The hard times were over... or so I thought.

*Chapter Ten*

# LIFE IS TOO EASY

ycling in South-East Asia is meant to be easy, with warm weather, beautiful beaches, cheap beer and fabulous street food. It sounded like a cyclist's dream, and what I had pictured this part of the trip would be like. Going over the mountains had been tough going, as was making our way across China, so I thought South-East Asia was going to be a bit of holiday in comparison. The aim was to enjoy our cycling, eat good food and relax in the sun.

Vietnam was different both culturally and in scale: we cycled past mini villages on rolling hills and purchased banh mi sandwiches for less than a dollar. There were little stalls and shops on every corner, selling every type of fruit or vegetable. It felt fun to be here and it was giving me my cycling mojo back.

It was day two of being in Vietnam, in the afternoon, and the sun was low in the sky. We stopped in a small café to try some of the local food. Having already sampled banh mi, I wanted to try another traditional dish, a soup called pho. We went past a restaurant selling different kinds of pho and stopped before going in and sitting down. The restaurant looked like a house inside with family pictures on the walls and six long wooden benches for customers to sit at. On each table were a set of chopsticks, toothpicks, along with salt, pepper, and chilli. We ordered two pho before sitting down to drink our accompanying beers.

Finola had to go to the bathroom. I sat there, excited for my meal, trying to speak to another customer in the restaurant but failing. She came back white as a sheet. I asked what was wrong, her face dropped and she looked like she was about to cry.

She told me, "There is a man back there cutting up a dog." I thought she was joking but the look on her face told me this was very real so I, too, ventured to the back of the restaurant, half in disbelief, half in morbid curiosity. As I walked past the thin curtain, I saw a man in denim overalls casually cutting the meat from a dog carcass laid down on the tiled floor. I could not bear to look at the dead dog, it's fur still attached. It was such a sad sight for my western eyes that I quickly moved away and ventured towards the toilet, where I saw three dog skulls sat in a bowl next to the entrance. Shock and amazement at the casual nature of the scene shook me. As I returned to the restaurant, the food was ready.

We could not bring ourselves to eat it after what we had witnessed. We understood it was our cultural sensitivity, but we did not want to eat dog meat. In an effort not to be rude, we tried asking what meat was in the soup. We made the sounds of chickens, cows and dogs but never got a reassuring answer, just lots of laughs from the Vietnamese customer at the back of the restaurant. We couldn't eat the meat in the soup and, although it certainly looked like chicken, we could only go as far as to drink the broth (which was still very tasty). We finished our beers before paying and making a quick exit. I had heard so much about the dog meat trade in Vietnam but I was shocked to find it so liberally on display. While I am aware that our two cultures treat the dog very differently, and I have no problem with the Vietnamese eating dog, I had a pet dog growing up and cannot separate the idea of eating the meat from the memories of our family pet.

We left the restaurant in shock and did not order any more food until we got to Hanoi and were able to translate the word 'dog'. (We also found out pretty quickly that we needed to translate cat and snake as well!) The road to Hanoi was pretty stressful, and the approach to the old town was the most difficult cycling of the whole trip. The sheer amount of motorbikes and traffic, which whizzed along continuously in every direction, combined with a road system without roundabouts or traffic lights, made it a relative death trap, which only worsened as we got closer to the centre. Once we were in Hanoi, with it's Franco-Asian food and 24-hour lifestyle, we realised it was an exciting city to spend some time in. We spent five fun-packed days here, trying all the beautiful Asian food from local food stalls, and spending the nights drinking beers in crowded bars, sitting in the centre of town on little stalls. It became a bit like a holiday. Since everything was so cheap, we did not have to worry so much about money and both of us really enjoyed this little break from cycling. Before we left we made time to visit the famous Hanoi bicycle collective shop which managed to get hold of some new Schwalbe tyres for us and even gave both bikes a clean.

Leaving Hanoi was just as busy and chaotic as arriving, and although we had an excellent time being city tourists, we found it tough to cycle in Vietnam. Even outside of the capital, there was too much traffic and far too many people. The little villages seemed to merge together, creating a super village, meaning there were no available wild camping spots as there are houses on every piece of available land. We had to find paid accommodation and, while we would often find a guest house for around seven dollars per night, it still ate up a large chunk of our daily budget. We had no income while we were away, so our small financial pot was decreasing daily, and this was putting a significant strain on both of us as we each wanted to spend money on different things. I wanted to live more cheaply but Finola, who was likely sensing that she would not see the tour out at this point, wanted to spend more of the budget on food, drinks and accommodation.

Vietnam is one of the cheapest countries we visited on the whole trip (with the cheapest beer at just 25p!) but we were spending more money here than any country before it. We could never agree on money as I wanted to make it last but Finola did not want to deny herself anything. I think we were both too stubborn to see each other's point of view. It did not help that we were drinking a lot to get along better, which would either be great fun or lead to big arguments. The only thing we had together was the trip, and it was important we kept going, so we decided to push on and venture into Laos, just south of Vientiane, and follow the Mekong River south towards Cambodia. The next few countries came fast, and we saw a lot in a short time.

Laos was beautiful, and the sun was really shining on us each day. It was considerably quieter than Vietnam with much less traffic on the roads. This made for quick and leisurely cycling, which we would combine with long lunch breaks to escape the heat. On one such lunch break, we stopped under the shade of a tree overlooking a muddy lagoon. We sat in the cool shade and began to make some noodles and, to our surprise, a large herd of oxen appeared out the bush on the other side and started wallowing and cooling off in the lagoon. The oxen were joined by horses and finally pigs: the animals had also come to cool off from the midday heat. It was funny watching them flip and flop in the mud before sloping off back into the bush, a lunchtime show.

Cycling south was relatively unremarkable, with the road across from the Mekong straight and flat which lent itself towards fast and direct cycling. We would often camp out in the old rice paddies since we knew these would make for safe and flat camping. Sometimes they had little wooden shelters, shady and raised flat platforms which were perfect for sitting and making our dinner.

The villages were much less densely populated than in Vietnam but they had everything you could want. Cycling past a small village one day, I was going quite fast on the hard ground and I heard a snap come from below me. I felt my bike become very bouncy and unstable. I stopped straight away to check out the problem. I looked down and, to my horror, saw that the right chainstay had snapped. This is an essential part of the frame which runs parallel from the cranks to the rear wheel. To break it was a total disaster as the bike was unrideable and needed fixing straight away. Calmly, I called out to Finola that we needed to turn back. We only had one option and that was to return to the village and try to find a welder to repair the broken bike. I had chosen a steel bike frame for this reason and knew if we could find a welder they would be able to fix the problem.

The village was small and consisted of a few small shops and two rows of houses which ran parallel to the road. We stopped at the first shop and asked them to help by showing them the broken frame and they pointed us to a small repair shack down the road. The hut was manned by a boy, aged 14, wearing a vest and sitting in a chair. We showed him the problem expecting someone else to come along but he understood and immediately turned the bike upside down and began to weld the metal back together. Sparks flew everywhere as the boy worked without even a face mask. It was a simple job but he proudly showed off his work, hitting the metal chainstay with a hammer to show me how it was now solid. He'd done a great job. When I asked him about payment he just wanted one dollar, I gave him three and he was both proud and very happy. I was very relieved, it looked rough but I was able to cycle again and my decision to purchase a steel bike proved to be a good one. I was also feeling very lucky that this had happened in Laos, where just about every village has a welder and we were able to get back onto the road after only an hour!

We continued along the Mekong towards Cambodia, reaching the border without any further issues. At the border the guard asked me to pay a dollar bribe, I resisted for about five minutes then got bored with the argument and paid him what he wanted. I guess my principles only last about five minutes!

Cambodia felt rougher than Laos. Busier, but poorer. The temperature increased as we crossed over the border, the ground went from brown to a rich orange colour. We had been in Cambodia for about two hours when we met a young Polish couple also on bikes, shopping in the small market in town. Their names were Chris and Monika and we spent the evening cooking dinner together with ingredients bought from the local market that morning. We even planned ahead and bought some eggs to have breakfast together the following morning. The next morning Chris said he would make scrambled eggs for everyone as Finola and I prepared coffee. The next thing we saw were eggs being cracked into a pan and blood coming out. It was horrible. We had accidentally purchased a dozen fertilised eggs, and each one contained a chicken foetus. Chris really wanted eggs so he checked each one, but each egg contained more blood. It was like a murder scene, and we all very quickly lost our appetites. You have to be really careful about what you are purchasing when buying anything in South-East Asia.

We split from our friends the following day. As they headed towards the capital, we took a more direct route to Angkor Wat. It was hot and humid with sweat cascading off our bodies. It made for uncomfortable cycling along the dusty, empty gravel roads, but we enjoyed the challenge and this was preferable to busier concrete highways.

The climate was taking its toll on me and although at the start of the day I felt strong and confident, my strength quickly started to fade. I was getting sapped of energy more and more each day and was unable to replace it. It felt like my batteries were running on empty. We were about 250 kilometres from Angkor Wat when this started and it meant that often I had to lie down in the shade to recover. Only by lying down could I gain back my strength. This got so bad as we approached Angkor Wat that I had to lie down about every 10 kilometres to regain my energy. Something was seriously wrong, but since we were in rural Cambodia, there was nothing we could do until I reached the big town of Angkor Wat, and I had to keep pushing through. Sometimes I had to lie down in the bush or crawl into abandoned buildings. Finola asked me to stop and rest, but I knew I could push on if I managed my reserves and took a few moments to recover. Looking online, the advice was that a rapid loss of energy like I was experiencing is one of the signs of malaria. I kept this to myself but inside I was worried as I knew malaria was commonplace here. I was absolutely shattered as we reached Angkor Wat and checked into a cheap room in town. I had to crawl to the bed to lie down as Finola went to get supplies. I did not know what was wrong. Perhaps I was under-eating or had picked up a sickness bug from somewhere, but once we had arrived in Angkor Wat things started to improve. I lay in bed and slept, with the fan trying to give me some comforting cooler air. I wanted to cool off further so Finola suggested we go swimming. We found a hotel which had a public pool and spent the day swimming, resting and eating. We stopped in Angkor Wat for four days to rest and visit the famous temples, and then when it was time to leave I had mostly recovered.

Leaving Angkor Wat, I felt stronger, and my energy was topped up. The rest and recovery had helped and we were off again to our next country, Thailand. It is a country that makes most of its money from tourism, with hundreds of thousands of tourists coming here every year to relax, party, shop and unwind. It's a paradise for some and as a touring destination, it is meant to be simple: cycle, eat, drink, sleep, repeat. I, however, found the mass tourism and ease of the country to be a negative and, for me, the land of smiles was tough going. I think perhaps I had convinced myself that this journey had to be difficult, with the lack of funds and gear over very high and cold mountain passes, and sleeping on a white sand beach just seemed to lack an element of adventure. Some people love it, and I don't want to discourage others, but to me it was not so great. Perhaps this is because I had been here twice before and so little came as a surprise. Everything was just too easy and convenient, and mass tourism created a distance between the local people and us: something we had not felt since we began the trip.

Cycling into Bangkok felt relatively safe and controlled. The traffic moved in a steady direction and, after the rushing and directionless traffic in Hanoi, it really was not bad at all. Thailand was also the place where we were due to meet my parents. They were coming out to Thailand for the first time to meet us and spend a week in the sunshine. It would be good to see them, and we planned to meet them in Phuket in the south of the country. This meant a steady ride of around 1000 kilometres over three weeks down the coast. Our average distance was 1500 kilometres per month so we were pretty confident we would make it in time.

Our ride out of Bangkok was as simple as getting into the city, and soon we were heading to the resort town of Hua Hin. This beach town was full of foreign expats living in their condos on the beach and, although nice, it did have a kind of tacky feel to it. We stayed in a small hostel run by a very large Dutchman, who must have weighed 25 stone and spent the day bobbing up and down in his pool while smoking a cigarette. I had previously stayed in the town at the large Hilton hotel on a work trip so I knew that you did not need a pass to get into the pool area. We grabbed our swimming stuff before casually walking past reception to the large swimming pool area outside and spent the day relaxing, swimming and reading in their beautiful five-star surroundings.

Carrying on from Hua Hin, we cycled down the coast before crossing over to the western side of Thailand and heading down the opposite coast towards Krabi and Phuket. It was simple cycling, with lots of beautiful beaches, and it was one of the few countries in which I was putting on weight rather than losing it as we were eating lots of cooked street meals and pastries from all the 7/11's dotted around the country.

On the approach to Krabi there is a small 500 metre hill, rising up over the limestone headlands before dropping back down onto the beach. As I was rolling down the hill, I heard the same crack and bounce that I had heard in Laos. I stopped, jumped off the bike, and saw my chainstay had snapped again. Luck was not so much on my side this time as I had to walk the 3 kilometres to the next village, while Finola went ahead and found a garage in which I could get my bike welded again. The young boy in Laos had done a temporary job, but this time we took it to a motorbike garage where they cut and re-welded over the old work and onto the steel. This looked a lot more of a professional job, and happily paid them £10 for the repair. With a stronger and more professional weld, I was sure it would last this time.

We got back on the bikes and spent a few days in the tourist town of Krabi. I found Krabi much like Bangkok, filled with backpackers and tourists having a great time. I looked around and felt out of place, that I was different. I had cycled here and, while I am sure they were having a good time, the more I cycled, the less I felt I had in common with the holidaying masses. I look back and when I went backpacking in 2012 to Thailand I had always felt happy to sit and chat with others, but the cycle ride was already changing me and I now felt more of an attachment to nature than to people. I wanted to explore the unknown and stay away from the mass tourist sites. We only stayed one day here as we had to get to Phuket to meet my parents, but I had seen enough. Krabi has much nicer beaches in the north, with simple wooden shacks and fewer people around. This resonated more with my current state of mind and the more I cycled, the more I realised I wanted to be away from not just civilisation and people, but Finola as well.

Our relationship was the toughest at this time, and we were arguing on an almost daily basis. This was not fun for either of us and I think we needed space, but that was impossible as we rode on. It became clear to me that the end was in sight, and I had to think about my options. What did I want to do? Go home and save our relationship or carry on alone? This was the central question going through my head, and I did not have an answer when my parents arrived in Phuket. Their arrival gave me additional time to stick my head in the sand and delay the inevitable.

It was great to see my Mum and Dad. It was quite impressive that they actually flew out to see us in Thailand as they had never been this far away from Europe before. It was a new cultural experience for them, and Thailand was an excellent way to start as you can still opt for western items on the menu if you choose. My parents had booked us our own room in a hotel with a swimming pool, it was the perfect upgrade from the tent, and we relished in telling stories over the Pringles and Dairy Milk chocolate that they had brought us.

We spent a week on holiday there, sitting on the beach, going to markets and going out for dinner. It was a fun experience to be able to see Thailand through their eyes. I think our trip and their experience of being in Thailand had a lasting effect on them, as not long after they booked a trip to Hong Kong and Australia, which really was pushing their boundaries. I think when they saw we were safe and having fun in countries which they previously considered dangerous or exotic, it made them believe that they could travel further afield too. We hoped that with our regular travel updates, others could see that the people of the world were treating us kindly without wanting anything in return, offering us acts of random kindness and hospitality. It was my intention for this trip to see if the world is a good place. If you watch the news and reports from the media most of what you see may be negative, since that is what sells. But my experience of the world was of the people who opened their homes and hearts, who shared food and beer, who just wanted to say hello. I reflected on this as we said goodbye to my parents and made our way towards Malaysia.

The short ride from Krabi to Malaysia took us about seven days, and it was clear that the religion in the area was changing. Thailand is mostly Buddhist, but in the south-east along the border with Malaysia, it becomes more

Muslim. "This is going to be really fun," I remarked to Finola, "Muslims are the friendliest people in the world, I think we'll be really welcome here."

As we crossed into Malaysia, the new country gave us some distraction from our problems, but this was the ending of us being together as a couple. Spending every moment together to this point in the trip had taken its toll, and we were unable to resolve our issues. We stopped talking, with both of us cycling in silence with headphones in until the end of the day when we could go to sleep. There was still some kind of love between us, but it had irrevocably changed forever.

I knew I had no desire to go back home, and that my future lay in unknown campsites and asphalt. It wasn't until we reached Penang, a beautiful island on the west coast of Malaysia accessible only by bridge from the mainland, that we finally made the decision to break up.

"What do you want to do?" I asked, while drinking a beer outside a small bar, "I don't want to go to Australia, I want to return home" Finola spoke softly. "It's too hot for me, I miss my friends and we aren't getting on anymore"

I agreed, "I think I'm going to stay, I want to finish this trip. Australia will be difficult, but I want to challenge myself and see what I am capable of."

We agreed that evening that we would book her flights home. It was sad but not unexpected. We had buried our heads in the sand for too long, and come so far together on our adventure, but now the only option left was to split up. We booked her flights from Kuala Lumpur and agreed to continue to the capital together as friends.

We had seen so much together and she had been so strong to come on this adventure, to test herself in a way many other people wouldn't, and I was proud of her. She had tried, she had lived, and while travelling together was hard at times, we had ridden from Reading to Kuala Lumpur together and formed a bond that will last a lifetime.

The last week of Finola's trip was uneventful, and we had a final camp out eating coconut ice cream, before a teary goodbye at the airport. I waved goodbye as she walked through the security gates, knowing she would be happy again, knowing a part of me had left and knowing I had to be better when I was on my own. A chapter of the trip closed as she turned and walked off, a turbulent, beautiful, adventure-filled year in which we both grew as individuals, even if we did not grow together. The humble bicycle had taught us so much – how to live freely, how to embrace life and most importantly, how to be happy. We had each found out so much together and I wished her the best, knowing she would be following me vicariously and I hoping she would keep the adventurous spirit alive in London.

*Chapter Eleven:*
# SOLO

The day after Finola flew out it dawned on me I was now on my own. It is quite the transition to go from being with someone every day to travelling solo. For eleven months we had shared a life, an adventure with all it's ups and downs and, while it was the right thing to separate, it still felt like I was now very open and exposed. So I did the only thing I knew to do, sat in a bar and ordered a beer.

The next day I organised my things and got ready to depart. I cycled 60 kilometres south out of Kuala Lumpur and it was a strange sensation to be cycling on my own, but in truth, I was enjoying it. There was a little bit more freedom in the decision-making, as I only had to answer to myself, and I opted for the route down the west coast. At first, it felt strange to eat alone in restaurants and I did not like sleeping alone in the tent, but I kept my head down, and with podcasts for company, I was starting to get the hang of solitary life on the road. I slept mainly in palm plantations and ate a lot of fruit and bread with Malaysian jam. I read a lot more. I rode at my own pace. I was starting to become stronger mentally, not because Finola was not there, but because being on your own forces you to make all the decisions yourself. You have no one to rely on so you must become better at doing the right thing the first time. I was already tough physically, as I had cycled from England to Malaysia, but I now needed to prepare myself mentally, as it would be an entirely different challenge now to the one of the last 11 months.

My legs were also getting stronger as I kept heading south. I cycled through plantations as the roads were quieter when one day a giant thunderstorm hit overhead. Electricity bubbled in the air and the rain, thunder and lightning cracked and whizzed just above me. It felt dangerous but exciting, as I knew that if anything happened to me here nobody would know where I was or what had happened. I was completely alone, and part of me enjoyed the feeling of isolation and vulnerability I had not felt before. I laughed out loud as I found shelter and watched the storm overhead, excited for the new life and the new road ahead.

I ventured south along the coast before turning sharply inland to head to the town of Kluang. I had a particular purpose in visiting here, as this was where my grandad was stationed in the Second World War. It was amazing to walk around a place where my grandad had been as a young soldier. I remember him telling me the story of his desire to join the fighting force in Malaya, as it was called back then, as he wanted to travel and see the world. Now, sixty years later, I was standing in the same place, exploring the same streets. When his regiment had asked if anyone had wanted to be stationed in Malaysia he volunteered straight away, without even knowing where it was. I think that I inherited his curiosity, wanderlust and 'say yes' attitude to travel. It felt like he was here with me, acting as my guide, as I walked around taking photos of the old hospital and railway to send back to him. To venture to a place that I had only heard about in his tales was magic, and I felt a real connection to him. As I tucked into the local speciality of grilled toast with a thick layer of coconut jam in the historic Railway Café, which had been in operation since 1938, I was sure Grandad Ted and his friends would have eaten the same in 1941. (The toast here was also the best toast I have ever tasted.) As I sat there, I thought of what he must have gone through during the war and was ever thankful for his service. The world is just a collection of memories and, in some lucky places, you can connect your story with that of someone you love. I was transported back home, to being a little boy and hearing my Grandad's stories from his council flat in Essex. I was able to match his past with my present, and as I sat in that station with a curious smile on my face I saluted him. Our paths were entwined together ever closer.

From Kluang, I cycled the two days to the border with Singapore and queued up in the busy motorbike lane to get my passport stamped. Ten minutes later, I was at the end of Asia. I was actually a day ahead of my scheduled booking at the famous bike touring hostel, Tree In Lodge, so rather than just cycle there I grabbed two beers from the local shop and went to drink them in the park. The sun was beating down on me as I drank my beers, and I was feeling like I had accomplished something real. I had reached the end of the road, the end of Asia. As I sat in the park, I reflected on my journey to this point. I missed Finola and I wished I had someone to share this success with, but I realised I was happier for being alone. As the humidity rose in the park, and the warm rain started to fall, I thought that I was still the luckiest person in the world to be able to be living and exploring every day, a life of freedom and opportunity.

The following morning I headed out of the park to stay at the Tree In Lodge hostel, a place that is famous among cyclists as it is run by the friendly and outgoing SK – who also offers half-price accommodation for anyone arriving by bike. He looked after me during the day as we swapped cycling stories, and Christophe, my friend from London who now lived and worked in Singapore, looked after me at night as we partied both in his house and out in the nightclubs of Singapore. It was a release of all the built-up emotion to be with someone from home with whom I could offload and reflect. We were often out until four in the morning and visited all the best nightlife Singapore had to offer.

After two days I was due to fly to Australia, I cleaned my kit: every inch of my bike, including under the mudguards, my sleeping pad and the tent floor. I even cleaned each tent peg, paranoid that the immigration services in Australia would fine me if anything was unclean. Everything was sparkling when I loaded my stuff into the cumbersome box.

I became nervous as I weighed all of my belongings and it came to 46 kilogrammes. Jetstar, the low-cost airline of Australia, had a maximum baggage policy of 40 kilogrammes. I was six kilogrammes over and looking at a $300 charge, so I was pretty nervous as I approached the member of check-in staff for my night flight at around 11p.m. I told her my story, that I had cycled all the way from England, and with a smile, she waved me on. With that, I was on my way to the great desert of Australia.

*Chapter Twelve:*

# ALONE IN
# THE OUTBACK

I arrived into Darwin airport at 4 a.m. It was dark and the still, hazy heat of the North Australian air hung over the airport as I put the bike back together. Once finished, it was around 5:30 a.m. so I headed over to the airport cafe and purchased the typical Australian breakfast of a coffee and meat pie. Once the sun came up, I was off to cycle 20 kilometres to the city centre to find a hostel open in the morning. At that time the roads were pretty clear, but it was such a change from the congestion and chaos of Asian roads, that it felt like I had the whole road to myself.

I arrived in the centre of town and found a small hostel where I coughed up the $35AUD for a single night. It was a bit of a shock to the wallet after being used to the low prices in South-East Asia. I quickly realised I had to get used to going back to the basics of cooking all my own food, camping and staying with hosts. Not to mention a new rule of no alcohol, otherwise my budget was going to get eaten up pretty quickly as each beer would now cost ten dollars.

I slept for a few hours before going on a quick walk around the city to visit the places I remembered from my previous visits to Darwin. Back in 2012, I was stuck in the city trying to sell an old car in which I had travelled from Perth to Darwin. The engine made all sorts of noises and the speedometer did not work, but I had no money so I could not leave Darwin until I sold the car. For nearly three weeks I stayed just north of the city in a squat located underneath an old house, with a collection of people living on sofas and mattresses in the hollow below, until I was able to sell it. I cycled back up the old road where I used to live, but disappointingly found the house fully renovated with none of the old characters living underneath.

That evening I sat in the corner of the hostel planning my route south towards Uluru and Adelaide, feeling content. Australia was going to be tough, and a direct contrast to what had made South-East Asia so easy. Desert conditions with little shade, long distances between food and water, huge unstoppable road trains and the infamous deadly animals. It would be just me and my bike riding across the most remote part of Central Australia completely alone; with no-one to help me if I got stuck, no-one to talk to if I got lonely, and no-one to blame if I did anything stupid. I was excited about touring once again, and that evening as I sat in the hostel and spoke with the other travellers about my past and upcoming journey, I felt energised for the road ahead. I had not been back to Australia since I lived there, and I felt a real sense of pride to be there once again, this time under my own pedal power. It had been five years since

I sat on that bus and sketched out a plan to cycle home. A re-birth of both self and ideas, and I had followed through. I had cycled from England to Australia and had tasted the freedom and independence that I had craved on that bus journey. I hoped that I inspired the same feelings in the people of that hostel as I sat there and told my stories. I knew that I was on the right track in my life and that track was about to take me south through the dangerous Australian outback.

The following morning, I got in contact with a WarmShowers host 40 kilometres south of Darwin who had offered to let me stay with him. WarmShowers is an online network of cyclists and like-minded folk, similar to couch-surfing, but aimed at touring cyclists, where the hosts provide a warm shower, a bed and usually some food. It is an amazing community and differs from couch-surfing as the hosts know that cyclists often arrive tired and likely in need of a shower, a good meal and rest, whereas couch-surfing is more about the partying. The network spans across the world but is most prevalent in Europe, USA and Australia. My host for the evening was called Kingsley, a man in his early fifties, tall, with short brown hair and a welcoming smile. I arrived and pushed past the steel gate which led to his home. On the gate was a hand-written sign which said "WarmShowers" so I knew I was in the right place. He showed me to an old barn that he let cyclists stay in, and we shared stories and a warm meal before departing in the morning.

That morning, I left around 9 a.m. and headed for the supermarket to stock up. Shocked at Australian prices after months of cheap eating, my shopping once again became the cyclist's staples of pasta, rice, noodles and oats. I loaded up with food and filled my eight-litre water sack which I hung on the back of the bike and set off for Kakadu. My first plan was to cycle to and around Kakadu National Park. This was adding about 300 kilometres of cycling in one of Australia's most beautiful national parks so was well worth the detour. The national park here has a charge of $40 just to enter, which I feel is justified to enable the park to be kept in pristine condition but since I was on a bike and had no emissions, I decided that it would be alright to just cycle in and cycle out. Luckily, I was never stopped or asked to show my ticket.

Kakadu National Park is known for being extremely remote, for aboriginal art thousands of years old painted onto caves, and for giant saltwater crocodiles. With this in mind, I made sure to camp away from creeks and rivers just in case. One thing I noticed when cycling into Kakadu was how hot it was. It was an oppressive dry heat that would suck the air out of my throat with the average temperature being over 40 degrees centigrade. I tried cycling through the midday heat on my first day out of Kingsley's house and was soon struggling. My exposed skin soon began to burn, and an unrelenting thirst meant I knew I had to stop. I knew I needed a new strategy for Australia and that strategy was simple: I would start cycling bright and early, between 11 a.m and 3 p.m I was going to rest, find some shade and wait it out, before pushing on again till nightfall when the temperature cooled. It was the same method Finola and I used in Kazakhstan. Luckily Kakadu has lots of bush camping and shrubland, so there is always somewhere to rest, even if it did mean lying underneath a small bush with only a few ants for company.

Apart from spending my afternoons peacefully lying under a bush, I soon learnt how dangerous Australia could be. I had just entered the national park area and was cycling to a camp area which was noted on my paper maps. As I cycled towards the spot, I noticed my water was getting low and I started to feel concerned. What if no water was available? How reliable were my maps? On arriving at a little roadside camp spot, I was happy to find there was a camping spot for me, no one else around and some picnic tables for me to have my dinner. Perfect, or so I thought as I turned the tap on the water tank and nothing came out. I had a look inside the tank, and there was nothing inside. I looked around the rest of the site and there was no water at all. I checked the maps and saw there was a petrol station about 60 kilometres away, but it would be too far to reach that day since it would be dark in an hour. I had to make a decision. I had two litres of water left, and although that would not last me if I cycled during the day, it might last if I departed first thing in the morning. In an effort to save my water, I had a dinner of bread and jam before going to sleep, and the following morning ate more bread rather than waste my limited supplies on my routine breakfast of coffee and oats.

I left just as the first rays of sunlight were coming over the horizon, and I had a mission. I had to cycle 60 kilometres to get more water or I would be in real trouble. I cycled with a purpose but tried not to overexert myself as I had to ensure I would not get too hot. My mind raced as I rode, thinking about what I would do if I ran out. Perhaps I could flag a passing car if one came by, though I hadn't seen a car all morning, or the day before; or the less appealing idea of filtering some water from a crocodile-infested creek. I watched the speedo tick off the kilometres and just hoped the petrol station was still there. I cycled at a steady pace while sipping my water carefully, and three and a half hours later, was relieved to see the colourful sign of a petrol station in the distance. Happy and relieved, I quickly filled up all my water bottles and was now carrying a total of 14 litres. I had been taught a lesson in self-reliance. Here I was on my own out in the middle of nowhere, and I was trusting a paper map which I had picked up for free in a tourist information centre in Darwin. This map could not know if there was water in the tanks. I had to be better prepared. Luckily, if I did get in real trouble with water here, I could stop and wait for a car to pass, but as I travelled further south, there would be fewer cars and I would have to be more careful, more conservative. I had to ensure I always had water; I could not trust the maps.

It was around 9 a.m. when I left that petrol station, loaded up with water, and having learnt a valuable lesson; I was just grateful nothing serious had happened. It is easy to be complacent, especially when you are so experienced, but each country brings a new challenge. This was an important start to my Australia adventure.

The rest of the cycle ride was beautiful. I saw aboriginal art on the rocks; painted pictures of naked men and red earthy handprints juxtaposed against a white chalky outline. The nature seemed more wild, more remote, with towering termite mounds and three metre high yellow speargrass all around me. I stopped at every creek to look for crocodiles but didn't see a single one which was disappointing, although there were plenty of signs to tell me they were around. This was my first long-distance solo cycle, and I was really starting to enjoy it. There was a real sense of safe exploration as I rode on between the diversity of nature and beautiful marked camp spots. I met a few other tourists here who seemed most surprised to see someone on a bicycle, thinking it was dangerous to cycle solo, one such tourist telling me straight up, "You're mad mate, it's your funeral". It was comments like this which spurred me to head further south.

As I came out of the national park, I finished my loop before heading towards Katherine. This was the first big town south of Darwin and meant I could restock my supplies cheaper here than in the provincial towns and petrol stations. The distance between Katherine and the next large town to the south was 650 kilometres, so I stocked up pretty heavily and bought lots and lots of food. I had cans of beans and plenty of different types of pasta. I definitely had something to learn here about the weight of my food, but as I left the store with two bulging carrier bags, I knew I could be self-sufficient for the next leg. My bike weighed around 75 kilogrammes at this stage with all the water and food I carried and I could feel the extra load as I pushed off towards Tennant Creek.

The ride south was lonely and my major regret was not recording a podcast diary as I had hoped to. I wanted to record something to not only document my thoughts and feelings, but to see if I would go a little stir crazy by cycling so far all alone. But instead, I found that after cycling 100 kilometres, often in strong headwinds, I was too tired to write or record anything. Usually, I would lie down on the dusty ground at the end of the day to rest and would stare up at the sky, unable to put my thoughts together. The cycling was often on flat, remote, featureless roads with large distances between any features or towns, and while it does not sound interesting, it started to become something I strangely enjoyed. I discovered a feeling which I like to call 'Cycling Zen'. It is like a moving meditation and I would often find myself getting into the 'zone' and time would fly by. I would be cycling and quietly enjoying myself, and I felt as if my legs were cycling on their own, pistons in the machine, propelling me forward as my brain cleared of any thought and the landscapes and time zipped past. I had never experienced this before, and it was a real bliss to be able to reach this meditative state. My mind was clear for the first time. I think this is what people call mindfulness and meditation and I only achieved this state when cycling alone. It would not happen every day, but would occur perhaps once or twice a week and seemed to come along when I needed it most.

Australia offered perfect camping with bush areas everywhere which lined both sides of the road, so before nightfall I would jump off the bike and push it 200 metres into the bush, entirely out of view of the passing vehicles. I could sit on the red dust, cook my meals in total silence and once night fell, I could look up at thousands of stars above. I would read outside by torchlight before I got too tired and I would go to sleep inside the tent. It was so idyllic and peaceful, and I was never disturbed by the snakes or dangerous spiders which reside in this part of Australia. I never really got lonely, especially once I got into it, and I think this is due in part to the blissful Cycling Zen I would achieve, as well as the fantastic natural campsites I found. In fact, sometimes I would rather camp in the bush than in the road rest stops where I would often find Australian 'grey nomads'. These were older people travelling in their caravans and campers. Sometimes I would stop just a few hundred meters in the bush away from the roadside stop since I preferred to be on my own rather than go in where I would attract lots of attention and then have to spend the whole evening telling people about the trip. The Australian people are lovely and would invite me for dinner or a beer with them over an evening, and often I would go, but sometimes I needed my peaceful sleep, the stars, the radio, my book and the silence.

Heading south, my target was Uluru since this was one of the tourist sites I had never visited when I previously lived here and I really wanted to see it. The road south goes past the famous hot water springs of Mataranka, which made for a beautiful warm water bath alongside bathing lizards. A perfect spot for a rest and a wash. Going further south I soon reached the milestone of Tennant Creek, which marked exactly one year on the road. It was an amazing feeling to know that I had been cycling for a whole year, and I celebrated the occasion with a cheeky beer in the local pub. I was drinking a lot less in Australia due to the prices of beer and being on my own meant I had little reason to, so I was feeling healthier both in body and mind.

As I headed south towards Tennant Creek, the weather started to turn and the warmer climes of the Northern Territory were giving way to the upcoming winter in the south. I would often wake up to temperatures of zero degrees and a small layer of frost on my tent since the desert warmth dissipates overnight with no cloud cover to keep the heat in.

Upon arrival, it was time to restock my supplies as I had eaten my way through all my tasty food and was only left with rice. It was good to have some emergency rice, but it always found its way down to the bottom of the bag as I prefer bread or pasta based meals. There was a large supermarket here, and I stocked up before cycling out of the town when I saw another cyclist. This was a person riding a road bike which was uncommon in this part of Australia, so I stopped and said hello. His name was Henri Manders and he was a Dutch man in his late fifties. We decided to go to the local fast food place for a coffee and got talking about cycling. It turned out that Henri was working in Cairns as a mountain bike judge for a big competition and he was in Tennant Creek for the night as he travelled by bus back south. Henri suggested we go for dinner later that night so I agreed and went with him to a local restaurant, where Henri told me he used to ride professionally as a racer and even won a stage in the 1985 Tour de France. I was having dinner with a cycling professional, and he told me about all his racing days. A chance meeting with another sporting hero, it was great to meet Henri, and he inspired me to ride ever faster the following day.

Leaving Tennant Creek, again with a full load of food and water, I cycled, not that much faster towards the next destination which was Alice Springs, 550km and another six days riding to the south. Although the nights were colder, the camping was just as impressive and being so isolated in the wilderness with the stars above me never failed to capture my imagination. Arriving at Alice, I stayed with another WarmShowers host for the night, in the pretty uninspiring state capital. I then continued along the road until I found the turn off for Uluru and the majestic red rock in the centre of the country. The road heads 90 degrees west, and this led to cycling into a consistent headwind, so I bought some extra food at the service centre and ventured towards the rock. The going was slower but not altogether horrendous, and I was making considerable progress.

About two days before reaching the entrance of the national park, I ran into another long-distance cyclist named Matteo, an Italian who was also cycling around Australia. He had curly black hair and had ten 2L water bottles stored in the front basket of his bicycle. We were going the same way, so we cycled together and spoke about travel and politics. Matteo was cycling around Australia to see the country as part of his working holiday visa. We both had the same views on distance and budget, so it made a good fit to see Uluru together. In Australia, I had thought I would be the only person who was cycling, but in the loop to Uluru, I saw eight different touring cyclists, most coming the other way. It was great to see so many people out on their bikes touring this great country.

Once Matteo and I reached Yulara, which is the main township of Uluru, we stopped for food and I bought biscuits and Matteo bought a four-litre tub of ice cream! We quickly ate our ice cream along with another touring cyclist, who incidentally, I would meet again on the road randomly in South America, where I would recognise him by his distinctive homemade denim gloves. Once we had eaten our fill of ice cream, which was all of it, we cycled up to the entrance of the national park, prepared this time to pay the $25 entrance fee. I took the lead and spoke with the young girl behind the counter, telling her our story about the bikes and how far we had travelled. Either she liked my story or took a fancy to me since she then let us all go into the national park for free!

All three of us then cycled the road that leads to Uluru. As we approached, we could see the red monolith rising up out of the ground. Eight hundred meters high of solid sandstone, the only visual interruption in 1000's of kilo-metres of flat desert. We stared upwards with awe and respect and took turns taking photos of us with the rock in the background. We then cycled around it before all agreeing that climbing it was not for us. People do climb, but the ancient aboriginal owners say it is offensive to step on the site and I think if it is offensive to a particular group of people, then it is best left alone. It is a magical place, and there is an energy much akin to a stillness that reminds you that you are such a small part of a massive world.

The best time to view the rock is at sunset and sunrise, but you usually are unable to stay in the park after hours. However, since Matteo and I had our bikes, we quickly pushed them into the bush, set up a camp hidden from view and were able to see the majestic sunset, orange and blue hues bouncing off the surface of Uluru.

The following day we cycled to Kata Tjuta, which is a smaller rock further away, before leaving the national park and heading back onto the highway. The difference this time was that the wind was blowing in our direction, it felt like we were flying, as we raced each other along the road. Once at the highway, we split ways, with each of us going in different directions. It was great to meet like-minded cyclists to share the road with, and this was the first time I had been cycling with anyone since Finola left. I enjoyed the company, and it made visiting the rock a much more social and shared experience, but back on the road, I was happy to be on my own again.

I continued south, knowing I was headed for the famous mining town of Coober Pedy. Coober Pedy is renowned for sweltering summers, so hot that everyone lives underground in little caves to keep themselves protected. The town is also famous for mining and is the main area where people mine for the Australian gemstone, opal. Upon my arrival, I stopped by the tourist information office to see if I could visit any of the underground houses and was pointed in the direction of a campsite about five kilometres out of town where campers could stay underground for $15, and also included a free tour of the mine there. Happy with my booking, I decided to go to the shop to buy some lunch to have at the campground. I left the information centre and cycled in the direction of the centre of town. It was only a short distance of less than one kilometre, and I did not put my helmet on for this short distance, out of pure laziness, and after about a minute I heard a loud woo woo sound and looked back to see the distinctive lights of a police car behind me. I knew instantly why I had been stopped.

Cycling without a helmet is illegal in Australia and carries a $300 fine. Annoyed with myself, I quickly thought how best to plead my case as I stopped. I was approached by a tall Australian policeman in his mid-thirties telling me off for cycling without a helmet. I told him my story about cycling around the world and that I had just come from the tourist office, but he was not budging. He sat there with a stern look, telling me of the dangers of crashes and asked for my ID. I pulled out my British driving licence so he could take down my name and address, and I asked for a smaller fine, telling him I could not afford the full penalty. As he was

*Top:* Leaving from outside the Reading Bicycle Kitchen.

*Middle*: Making quick progress across Europe.

*Bottom*: It wasn't all sunshine: rain in Romania.

**Top left:** Zida (left), Melih (middle) and Burek (far right).

**Middle left**: The Dangerous Section!

**Bottom left**: Sandy roads in Kazahstan.

**Bottom right**: Changing money in Uzbekistan. This is $100 worth.

**Top right:** Beautiful Bukara. Unfortunately, I was sick so stayed mostly in the hotel.

**Middle right:** Reaching the top of the pass in Kyrgyzstan, surrounded by snow.

**Top left:** The most beautiful road, Kyrgyzstan.

**Left**: Sharing a teabag in a tea house in the mountains.

**Bottom left**: We were a stong team over the mountains.

**Top right:** Entering China.

**Right**: Road workers who saved us from the Hami Hurricane.

**Bottom left**: It was much more interesting in Southern China.

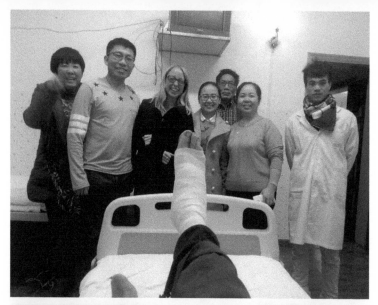

**Top left:** My rescuers! *L–R:* Rico's Mum, Rico, Finola, Rennie, Rico's Dad, Lu and Xi.

**Middle left**: getting my bike back together in Laos.

**Top right:** Feeling tired and listless in Cambodia.

**Bottom right:** There were limited opportunities for resupply in Australia.

*Top:* Uluru

***Bottom:*** Perito Moreno glacier

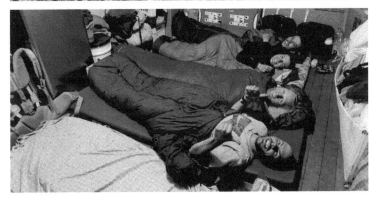

***Top left:*** 30,000 km marker, reached in Southern Chile.

***Top right:*** With Kenneth in Bolivia.

***Middle left***: Home for the night.

***Middle right:*** Bolivian Lunch spot.

***Bottom left:*** Making friends in Sucre. *L–R:* Isreal, Me, Ellen, Pim and Marie.

***Bottom right:*** Sleeping in the Casa in Pitumarca. *L–R:* Me, Kenneth, Morgane and Greg.

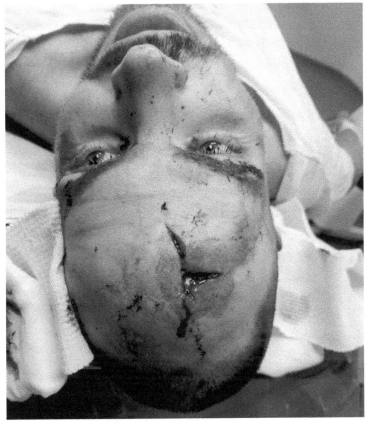

***Top left:*** Reaching Rainbow
Mountain with Greg and Morgane.

***Middle left***: Cycling up to
Ausengate.

***Bottom left:*** Smiling at 4950m
in Peru, the highest elevation
I cycled on the trip.

***Top right:*** Crossing the equator
for the final time, Ecuador.

***Bottom right:*** About to go
into surgery.

**Top left:** Reunited with Kenneth and Marie in the brothel hotel.

**Middle left:** Head is sewn up but the bike did not make it.

**Bottom left:** Hiking the Acatenango volcano.

**Top right:** Riding the very steep hills of Guatemala.

**Bottom right:** Riding in Florida with Leif and Ashley.

*Top:* The final 100m of 46,500km.

*Middle*: I Did It! Greeted by my mum and dad at the pagoda in Reading, PA.

*Right:* Big hugs all round on my arrival.

*Photo credit: Susan L. Angstadt / Reading Eagle.*

looking at my driving licence, he started to smile and asked me where in Reading I was from.

Bemused, I told him "I live three miles out of the centre, in Earley, on the way to Wokingham."

He laughed and added "My wife is from Wokingham. I've been to Reading many times."

"So we are almost neighbours," I added. The policeman looked over me and the bike and added "I'm going to let you off with a caution, but only due to the local connection. You must wear your helmet at all times. There are no excuses."

"Thank you, it means so much." I replied "I won't do it again."

The Reading connection saved me, and I was relieved as I popped my helmet back on, and cycled the five kilometres to the campsite. I was shown to what looked like an underground bunker, with a concrete floor and although it was a nice gimmick, I preferred to be outside so I sat on the picnic bench outside and enjoyed a glass of wine with my lunch while I laughed at how I had just got away without a hefty fine. What a small world!

Riding south from Coober Pedy meant I was now deep into the South Australian heartland and as I cycled ever closer to the coast, the colour of the ground had gone from red, to yellow and now to green. It was a clear sign that I was approaching the agricultural home of Australia. At times it was almost more like cycling around the rolling plains of

England than barren Australia, with cows and sheep lined up and saying hello to me through their fences. I cycled past places where I used to live with Nick back in 2012, including Gawler and Mallala, as I realised I had cycled to a place which had previously taken me a 24-hour flight followed by a 20-hour drive to reach.

In what felt like no time I had reached Adelaide, 3300 kilometres and just over two months south of Darwin, where I stopped for two days to rest and recover. As I arrived, I noticed a crack had appeared on my rear wheel rim. While cycling down the centre of the country, I would often ask my bike to just get me to Adelaide. I would stroke the top bar and say, "just another thousand kilometres", and it seemed to listen, with the only real problem being a snapped front rack which was fixable with cable ties. Easily repairable in Adelaide, I was quite proud of how the old wheel had made it 24,000 kilometres and nearly 400 days without a problem.

A few days in one place also gave me time to reflect that, like my bike, I had made it across the desert. I had cycled through the heat and isolation, I had avoided snakes, spiders and crocs while I bush camped and lived on my rations of both food and water. I wanted to make it to Adelaide, and like my bike, had come out of the desert unscathed and with a new knowledge that I could cycle alone, be self-sufficient and most importantly, I enjoyed it. Cycling on my own was fun, although there were times when I was having dinner or sitting watching the sunset when I wished for company.

When cycling, it is simply better alone. You are not concerned with anyone else, your decisions only have an impact on yourself, and you have a greater degree of freedom. I learnt a lot more about myself by cycling solo for three months than in the previous eleven months on the road. I had discovered my cycling Zen. I also had the chance to meet people like Henri, who I might not have met had I been in a cycling two-some. The desert was meant to be a test, and I had passed. I had made it to Adelaide and I guess one of the reasons I never made that podcast to capture my declining mental state was that it did not decline. If anything, it went the other way and I was stronger mentally knowing I could conquer anything.

With the rim repaired, it was time to depart from Adelaide and head to Melbourne to cycle along the Great Ocean Road, a beautiful stretch of highway linking Portland to Torquay at the bottom of South Australia. It was a beautiful road with tall eucalyptus trees lining the forest roads with views over the Southern Ocean as you climb the steep, sharp climbs. The road bends back onto itself, revealing a new view with every turn. It was a marked difference from the straight flat desert roads of the Northern Territory. I had actually driven this road twice, but cycling gave me the time and freedom to take in the scenery that driving never does, even if the climbs are surprisingly steep by bicycle. I even saw a koala walking along the ground, a beautiful sight as the young bear calmly climbed into the hinterland before me. An experience I would never have seen by car.

My budget was getting low. I had expected the original money I had saved to last over two years, but after one year I had only around £800 left in the bank account and I knew I had to find work. In New Zealand, I could qualify for a working holiday visa which is a short term work visa meant to supplement your travel. I applied for the visa, and this was quickly approved. I contacted my old employers, Flight Centre, as they had offices in Auckland, and managed to secure an interview once I arrived in the country. This was a weight off my shoulders, and I knew that I would have some money coming in once I got there.

My final cycling destination in Australia was Melbourne, where I would be welcomed by my friend Dylan and his wife-to-be, Nicole, and their dog Ripley. It was great to rest and relax with them for two days while I recovered from the road, and it was good to catch up. We used to work together in London, and those bonds last a long time. From Melbourne, I had only a few days to reach Sydney before my flight to New Zealand, so I took a night train to get there. Annoyingly, I had to box my bike to go onto the train, so I left for the train station early to get that done and then headed to Sydney.

In Sydney, I stayed with my good friend Lynsey who I met down at Bondi Beach. I must have looked quite the sight in front of all the lifeguards and beachgoers as I waited to meet her in my waterproof trousers and stained and ripped hoodie! It was great to see her again. She was my old boss at Flight Centre back in the UK. She was a big supporter of my new path, and it was fun to catch up. We celebrated with beer and bottles from her extensive wine collection. She was a great host and would let me chill for the two days I needed to prepare for New Zealand and get ready to start a new life. A working life.

After arriving in Auckland, I was quickly reunited with the world of work, and after a quick interview and familiarisation with the same systems used in both New Zealand and the UK, no further training was required. I was sent straight to work for three weeks in a store on the high street before moving to a local store in the Broadway area.

The adjustment was possibly too much too soon for me, and while it was fun to meet new people and tell them my stories, I did struggle to sit still behind a desk and work day in, day out. I had gone from seeing something new every day to seeing the same office daily. I rented a small apartment, and in just one week, I had gone from cycling solo in Australia to being back in the office, wearing a shirt and sitting on a comfortable chair. There were times when I wanted to run away and head back to nature. It was a very quick transition, and it would have been better to adjust more slowly rather than jumping straight into it, but I needed the money, especially since New Zealand is a very expensive country.

It took around three weeks to get back into the swing of the working life, and it helped to work with some outstanding people around me. I was lucky to be able to work in a really fun and vibrant team in Broadway, with Edel, Amber, Fran and Martyn. We all bonded very quickly and would often go on work socials together. Edel and I clicked the most, and we became very close friends. Both of us like an after-work drink and we would often sit around the office and talk over a bottle of red. She was my rock and made the transition into life in New Zealand much easier for me. She also made it hard for me to leave. I felt we were close, and I started to fall for the red-headed Irish lady, but nothing ever happened. My heart fell in two places, but the road was calling once again. I could never tell her how I felt as I knew that one day soon I would leave as I had a journey to finish. I knew I would miss her but I also missed the road, the freedom and adventure of travelling by bike. I had another difficult decision to make.

I could do one of two things. I could stay in New Zealand. I had a job, a flat and life was good. I had friends, stability and the possibility of romance, but on the other side there was the rest of the world calling. In my downtime in the office, I would look at pictures of Patagonia and other places in South America, which would make my pulse race and my heart jump. The landscapes of Southern Argentina and Chile were just calling to be cycled through. Perito Moreno Glacier, El Chalten, Fitzroy. The scenery looked perfect, and when the tour is calling, I am not one who is able to resist the call. I secretly booked the tickets in November and told my colleagues in December, and then my boss, who was again very happy for me to leave. I hoped this was more of a reflection on those people who want to watch a real life adventure unfold than on a poor work ethic! I booked two flights, one from Auckland to Buenos Aires and then another from Buenos Aires to Ushuaia.

Ushuaia is known as the bottom of the world, located on the very southern tip of Argentina. It's a small port town from where many boats leave for Antarctica. A town famous for being isolated, cold and very windy. You have to time your arrival right as otherwise it will be too cold, and a lot of the roads and ferries will be closed for the winter. I chose 1st February to start as, although a tad late in the season with most cyclists arriving in December or January, it still meant it would be rideable, and it would give me that extra month of pay.

I was excited to continue the trip, and I knew that flying to South America was the right thing to do. I had learnt about riding solo in Australia and therefore was able to take that experience and match it to the wilds of South America. My last month in New Zealand was spent with Edel and my friends from work. I was living out of an AirBnb hostel which was the cheapest accommodation in Auckland, and it was sad to say goodbye to some amazing people, but I looked forward to the road. I had learnt that I needed to be outside, to be on the right path, to be seeing new things but I was also sad to leave the connection and community which I had built up. Change, however, is essential, and I knew I would once again be living my most authentic life.

*Chapter Thirteen*

# PATAGONIA

I t was a 13-hour flight from Auckland to Buenos Aires, and during that time, I drank five gin and tonics in fast succession before the air steward came to me and said I could have no more. I was getting my money's worth on the expensive flight as I headed to Patagonia with its wild winds and remote lands. I was also a little nervous as it would be the first time I had travelled alone where English is not the first language. I had once again left behind a routine that offered a relative degree of stability, a life considered 'normal', for a life of nomadic uncertainty.

Before arriving in Ushuaia, I had booked a stopover for a few days in Buenos Aires to gradually introduce me to South America and to be able to see the beautiful capital of Argentina. Upon my arrival into Buenos Aires Airport, I wheeled the bike along with the luggage to the coach station where they were happy to load everything into the bus to take me into the city. When I arrived, I unloaded the bike box and bags and went to look for a taxi to take me to the hostel, but quickly and very sternly I was told. "Do not leave your things there, they will be stolen. Behind that wall is a Barrio." A Barrio is a slum area of Buenos Aires and the bus station was located directly next to the Barrio, behind a large, graffiti covered wall. I had been pretty complacent with my belongings and safety so far on my journey. However, I now had to remember that there are some areas of South America which are less safe than other parts of the world. The guards at the bus depot were very helpful and they called a taxi for me whilst I stood and waited next to my luggage, my bike enjoying a well deserved rest in its trusty box.

The taxi took me to a small hostel which from the outside looked like a large townhouse. I knocked on the door and I was greeted by a beautiful Latin lady with long flowing brown hair and dark eyes who welcomed me in. The place was alive with activity and chatter, and I felt welcome straight away. The hostel staff were really interested in the bike trip and allowed me to store my bike in the main hallway so I did not have to unpack it. This was a relief and I was able to get on with being a tourist in Buenos Aires.

I enjoyed a few days of relaxing and sightseeing in the capital, taking in the cobbled plazas and patios of the Palermo district. But soon I found myself on another four-hour flight to the southern tip of Argentina. It felt important to me to start at the bottom of the continent and work my way northwards, and with my destination as Reading, Pennsylvania, the only way was up. I would point my bicycle north for the first time since I began the trip, and I would be able to look directly at the finish line of my adventure, albeit still 20,000 kilometres away. It also meant that I was free again after the hustle and bustle of city life in Buenos Aires. I would be back on the open road with the wind in my face and sleeping out in the open where I was truly happy.

Upon arrival in Ushuaia, I could barely contain my excitement as I rebuilt the bike in the tiny building which resembles more of a log cabin than an airport. Ushuaia is a small town looking out over the Beagle channel. There was a strong wind blowing in my face as I cycled the barren and wild 10 kilometres from the airport to the town. I took the two obligatory photos, one in the harbour with the Ushuaia sign and one in the national park some 20 kilometres south of Ushuaia which is the most southern road in the world. It was great to cycle in the national park and the beauty of the wilderness was abundant. I camped there for free beside a beautiful river and climbed the glacier the following day. I was already being blown away by Patagonia. There was a freedom to the openness of the landscape. Clear water seemed to bubble out of the ground and rush down past vibrant green grassland, which contrasted beautifully with tall white-peaked mountains in the background. It made such a contrast to the city life in both Auckland and Buenos Aires.

I much prefer life outdoors and find that it calms me just being outside. When I am cycling, I only have to worry about three things: where I am going, what I am eating and where I will sleep. In the real world, the working world, you have a constant barrage of information you must process. Hundreds of little packets of information which make demands on your time and energy. Decisions which must be made and things which can cause you anxiety and stress. I prefer the simple life. It allows me time to think, to understand, to truly reflect on myself and my surroundings and to be genuinely reliant on myself for everything from sustenance to entertainment. Just being in the natural world has the effect of a calming meditation, which I found was missing during my time in Auckland. I was pleased to be back on the rough roads of Patagonia and happy to once again test my levels of fitness against the world.

When I am working hard in a city, I find I can become easily distracted and depressed. I find myself reading less and thinking less. I sit in front of the TV, and I overeat. I am lazy. I get fat. When I am outdoors, I am again flooded by endorphins, and the thought of cycling great distances fills me with the anticipation and excitement of a great adventure. This is why I found myself at the bottom of the world, looking up, with the aim to just get to the end of each day, wherever that may be. To be excited by a new camp spot, to look around me at new surroundings rather than down onto a computer screen. To be responsible for every single decision I would make, to be accountable for living, to be free.

The challenge to cycle north from Patagonia was going to mean slow progress, since this region is famous for a constant, intense headwind which blows straight from the north, and straight into my face. It was as if the wind was trying to hold me back from my goal, but I was strong and stubborn and pushed on regardless. Leaving my camp spot on that first day in the national park, it was cold and windy, and I was soon in the full force of nature with the wind blowing some 40–50 kilometres per hour in my direction. I only cycled around 45 kilometres that day as I looked to regain my fitness and I found a beautiful campsite north of Ushuaia just after the first pass. The next day, and only 60 kilometres away, (but an eight-hour ride due to the wind) I arrived at my first Casa de Ciclista in South America. A Casa de Ciclista is a house or property which welcomes cyclists. It is like the WarmShowers network, but you do not need to contact the host beforehand, you can just arrive and say hello, or in this case, "Hola!"

This casa was located inside an Argentinian bakery in the centre of the little town called Tolhuin. I was quite nervous about asking to stay, not knowing how the system works. I entered the bakery and purchased a coffee and a small Argentinian cake called an alfajor, which is similar to a biscuit we have back in the UK called a Wagon Wheel, with two pieces of sweet biscuit held together by jam and coated in chocolate. I sat there eating my treat with my helmet on the table signalling my intention to stay. When I had finished, I walked up to the counter and tried to explain my intention to stay at the bakery, but since I knew no Spanish, I simply stood with my helmet in my hand and a hesitant smile on my face. The guy working behind the counter understood and got another member of the staff to guide me around to the back of the bakery. I followed him with my bike, and we walked into a small room which led to a huge warehouse. Inside were six cyclists, all welcoming me, saying hello in both Spanish and English.

I was shown to a room which had been graffitied by all the passing cyclists before me and contained two sets of bunk beds. I took a spare upper bunk and dumped my things down before going to meet everyone. There was a real mix here of South American and European cyclists, and everyone was going south. It seemed that not many people liked to battle the wind. We all sat around talking, with me trying to understand and generally failing when the language switched to Spanish. We shared an Argentinian delight called Dulce de Leche, a creamy sweet caramel and milk spread famous in Argentina. It came in a small tub like a jam or peanut butter and was packed full of calories. I took lots of inspiration and ideas from my fellow cyclists who had cycled the roads before me, and gained lots of useful information about winds, road conditions, camping and places to see. In South America, especially in the south, the cycling community is vital, and often when I saw someone coming in the opposite direction, we would stop and share information about the road ahead or behind.

The strong community spirit was a continual joy, and everyone I met I found friendly and accommodating even if I struggled to communicate. My lack of language skills did mean I was missing out on lots of topical and exciting conversation with the local people. This was very frustrating, especially since a lot of the farms I passed were willing to accommodate passing cyclists, but I did not want to burden them with my poor language skills. It was a shame and something I did work on as I went on, but at the beginning, I had no confidence in my ability to speak and therefore did not really try. I preferred to rough it and camp out, but since the wind would not let up, camping became a test to find the best wind protection. This would often be a disused or abandoned barn or building usually with a broken corrugated metal roof which would flap and bang and keep me up all night!

There is a constant headwind in Patagonia which blows all the way from El Chalten to Ushuaia over a distance of 1000 kilometres, meaning I would often cycle for eight hours and only cover 40 kilometres. This was especially noticeable when I crossed into Chile for the first time. There was a gravel road between San Sebastian and Porvenir, slowing me further, as cyclists flew past me at 40 kilometres per hour in the opposite direction, looking very happy with themselves. I discovered a masochistic side of me which wanted to feel the struggle and hardship of adventure. Often policemen or people in pickup trucks would stop and offer me a lift, but I was always too stubborn and said no. It is not like I was trying to cycle every mile, but I did enjoy the challenge of cycling into the winds. I felt that it was me versus the world and it also helped me to quickly get back into full fitness.

I had to keep cycling as this was the only thing keeping me warm, and the wind was making listening to music impossible, so I had a lot of time to enjoy the slow push forward. When it was time to camp, I slept the contented sleep of someone who had worked hard and achieved their goal for the day. I had to get more and more creative when camping and more than once I would jump off the road and climb into a storm drain beneath it. These are about three feet high and four feet wide, so I would get on my hands and knees and unroll my mattress and sleeping bag before climbing in, with only enough space to lie down. I would have a pretty sound sleep. I never saw any rodents, but it did make for a pretty nervous first hour with cars passing just three feet above my head.

Each day I would cycle until I was too tired or hungry to continue, and then head for the first barn or windproof area to stop. This kept the spirit of adventure alive and meant that I never knew when the day would end or where I would sleep that night.

Heading north in Patagonia, you continuously jump between the borders of Chile and Argentina and luckily, British passport holders do not have to pay to cross. The Chilean border guards are much stricter than the Argentinians, and they will not allow any fresh food or meat to be carried over the borders. The best thing to do is to put anything you do not want to be discovered at the bottom of your pannier, and then keep a low-value food such as an onion or some carrots at the top. I would always then declare my low-value vegetables and hand them over if asked and would not mind if these were taken away. With this strategy, they would not check my bags and discover my expensive cheese or salami, and sometimes I would even get my onion back.

Often, I would find a hostel in the larger towns and enjoy some of the famous Chilean or Argentinian wine while resting after battling the winds. Most hostels would offer a camping spot in the garden for around five dollars a night which fitted my budget and lifestyle. It was also an opportunity to meet fellow cyclists, walkers and hitch-hikers and chat about our experiences. Patagonia seemed to attract like-minded adventurous folk.

On rest days I was able to totally rest both my body and mind, which enabled me to let go of the battle to push forward and just soak in everything I had seen on the road before me. The main towns are called Puerto Natales and Puerto Arenas, and I stopped for two days in both of these little cities and ate a lot of delicious Chilean bread with a glass of good red wine which could be purchased in a box for just a dollar. My original plan was to take time off the bike to hike around the Torres Del Paine National Park but was put off by the high ticket price and expensive enforced campsites. One backpacker who completed the famous W trek told me he called it the "Torres Del Paine in the Ass" for all its red tape and high costs. It did look like a beautiful national park and something I wanted to cycle around, but I did not want to get caught out without paying. With the large number of cyclists here, who are known for their cost-cutting ways, I would have stood out, and I was happy to leave something to explore for next time.

I did, however, visit the Perito Moreno Glacier and it was one of the most beautiful natural sites I have ever seen. I took a spot in a campsite just outside the national park, left my bike and belongings and went to try to hitch-hike to the glacier. After waiting for around 40 minutes and not getting a lift, I was bored and cold and didn't want to wait any more so I went back to the campsite and decided to cycle there the following day. The route to the glacier required cycling back into the wind for 75 kilometres and it took me all day to reach the entrance, so I decided to camp there and visit the glacier the following morning.

I woke up to the sharp, cold blue skies and cycled in to visit the glacier. What I saw took my breath away. It is one of the most beautiful natural things I had ever seen. A thirty-metre high crystal clear wall of white ice rearing out of the water, with icebergs scattered all around. Occasionally a piece of moving ice would crash off the front of the glacier and come cascading down into the still water below with an almighty bang. There was respect and awe from the visiting tourists and the immense size of the white wall juxtaposed with the bright blue water, made this an incredibly memorable experience. It was truly majestic, and I had never seen anything like it. After cycling halfway around the world at this point, there are times when I thought I did not need to see the tourist sights as I felt I had seen it all. But this was a new feeling, this was a scene of pure beauty. The silence interrupted by the crash of ice sent shivers down my spine, loaded with excitement and wonder. I left the glacier buzzing, with a new respect for the power of mother nature.

I quickly cycled back to the town El Calafate where I spent another night in the campsite as I was not ready to leave this magical place. The next day I headed towards the town of El Chalten, a cute little mountain town at the footsteps of Mount Fitzroy National park a few days ride away. On route to El Chalten, I was being battered by strong side winds which meant I often had to stop and rest as the whole bike was being pushed sideways into the roadside ditches. I took shelter one night in a tiny storm drain, just big enough for me, my roll mat, and my sleeping bag before reaching the pretty mountain town.

Upon my arrival I cycled up the small, two-lane main street and bought some cakes to celebrate getting there, before finding the little Casa de Ciclista in the north end of town. This casa was run by a lady called Maria. She was a short, cheerful woman who lived in the house with her small family. She spoke no English but welcomed me in and informed me through sign language that she allowed cyclists to sleep in her garden and use her kitchen. There were 12 of us there at the time, all cyclists or hikers, and if you wanted to go hiking she would let you leave your belongings there free of charge. I camped on the first day and stocked up for my three-day mountain hike to see Mount Fitzroy. Most people hike the national park with backpacks and walking poles, but since I did not have any of that equipment, I loaded up my two rear panniers with food, stove and camp gear before popping my tent under my arm and went hiking. I must have looked a little out of place compared to people with all their fancy European equipment as I was often stopped and asked "what I was doing out here without a backpack?" I told them, "I don't own one and didn't want to miss out, so just carried everything like this. It works."

I wanted to complete the hike and knew I was strong enough to carry all my stuff with me. It was only approximately 10 kilometres of beautiful hiking each day to reach the free campsites, which I could cover in about three hours. I would set up camp before heading out to walk along the viewpoints and ridges of Mount Fitzroy. The sharp peaks of Fitzroy stood proud before the blue lake below and just as I got to the top of the mountain, the clouds cleared and all three mountain tops became visible. I stood alone and enjoyed the serenity of a place so far away from my previous lifestyle. I hiked alone but met and spoke with campers around me every night and there was a real sense of community here. There is something special about mountains and being so far away from our regular lives that it brought us all together in a shared experience. Everyone there could forget about their everyday lives, walk and talk in harmony in this beautiful environment. We were the audience to the show of Mount Fitzroy, and with each passing day, we were all falling more in love with the awe-inspiring nature around us.

The next border crossing was the most difficult and logistically challenging of the whole trip. I was to cross from El Chalten in Argentina to Villa O'Higgins in Chile. Firstly, you take a boat across a large lake called Lago Desierto before hiking across 15 kilometres of single-track woodland with the bike, then taking another boat across Lago O'Higgins where you will reach the town and the start of the famous Carretera Austral gravel road in Chilean Patagonia. My initial plan was that I was not going to cross this border due to the high costs of the boats. Since there is only one boat which takes passengers across, they can charge what they like. I was trying to make my money last as I still had a long way to go but my lovely sister, Linny, heard I was going to skip this famous crossing and sent me the money for the trip. She really helped me out as it meant I could continue on the same route as the intrepid cyclists before me.

On my way to the first crossing I met a Belgian cyclist called Alain, and we agreed to tackle the crossing together. We arrived at the small port, eager and excited to start, only to find that we had missed the boat that day. Disappointed and slightly downbeat we had some food and started to prepare ourselves for a night at the port when a boat pulled into the harbour. We spoke with the captain who agreed to take us over the first lake if we paid cash, and we quickly packed away our stuff as he was keen to leave straight away. It was a beautiful 30-minute boat ride over the icy blue waters of Lago Desierto surrounded by mountain peaks and forests. Upon our arrival on the other side of the lake, there was a small Chilean guard office where our passports were stamped, before being told we could camp out in the woods over to the right-hand side away from their office. This was perfect as it was getting late and we did not want to have to carry the bikes over the single-track hills after nightfall.

We met an adventurous hiking couple also taking this route and sat with them until it got too cold and we all retreated into our tents. The following morning, it was raining so we packed up quickly before starting the hike.

The single-track path was too steep and rocky to cycle, so we hiked and pushed our bikes through eight kilometres of soggy mud. I was very grateful to Alain for helping me push my heavy bike up the steep hills at the beginning as my tyres were too slick and my brakes not strong enough, which meant I kept sliding back down the muddy hill to the bemusement of the hiking couple behind us. It was a fun and adventurous border crossing where we had to cross three log bridges and remove our socks and shoes to push the bikes through two freezing cold glacial streams.

The remoteness of this crossing added to the excitement, and although it was slow going, I was enjoying the experience and company. Alain was a happy-go-lucky Belgian with the same sense of curiosity about the world as me. He was on his own journey to Vancouver, and we put the world to rights as we crashed and smashed our bikes over the wet and rocky terrain. It took us four hours to cross this hike-a-bike section before we reached the Chilean side, which was denoted by just a sign welcoming us back to Chile. The track then became much more manageable and we were able to cycle the 15 kilometres down to the next boat, which was scheduled to leave at 9 a.m. the following day. That night we planned to camp in a small campground overlooking the port, and as we cycled in, we spotted the young hiking couple who somehow had actually managed to beat us there. We enjoyed a relaxed evening and were welcomed like heroes for hiking our fully loaded bikes through the tracks.

The second boat took about two hours and was a pleasant cruise to Villa O'Higgins over more beautiful blue water alongside tall and commanding glaciers. Upon arrival, we had to visit the police who checked our passports and wished us well, before being allowed to cycle into the small town of Villa O' Higgins. We stocked up on delicious homemade bread and jam, and ate a little lunch in a park. Neither Alain nor me wanted to pay for camping, so we cycled out of the town after saying goodbye to our hiking friends. We cycled 40 kilometres of beautiful Chilean gravel road in just a few hours, finding that the big difference on this side of the glacial range was that the wind had stopped and we were able to cycle 40 kilometres in half a day rather than a full one. We cycled past a massive lake and I wanted to stop, to camp in front of this beautiful lake, and enjoy this taste of Chile with the calm winds and stunning views. Alain wanted to carry on and make some distance as he had a time limit to get to Vancouver. Everyone is on their own tour and it is essential to make the right decisions for yourself. We had shared a great little adventure as part of our own bigger trips, and it was fun to travel together for a few days, and we left each other as good friends. The following morning I awoke in my beautiful campsite with a desire to cycle the Carretera Austral and enjoy this beautiful and famous road.

The Carretera Austral runs from Villa O' Higgins north to Puerto Montt. It is 1000 kilometres long, mostly unpaved, apart from the northern end and the area around Coyhaique, which is the main town of the region. It is a beautiful road, but it is hard going since much of it is uneven and unstable and I found myself bumping along often with more frustration than enjoyment. While the road was tough on the body, the views were a treat for the eyes. The environment is similar to a rainforest with lots of green palms lining the road and plenty of freshwater found in the fast running glacial streams running next to the road. The road is varied, with enough gradient to make it an interesting ride, and the lakes which you cross by boat are crystal clear. I did not, however, enjoy this region as much as I had expected. Perhaps I had been spoilt by quieter roads in Kyrgyzstan or South China or Romania but I found this to be quite a busy road with a lot of tourism for a place which is known as a remote wilderness. I was seeing perhaps ten cyclists every day. With so many people, there was not the same close community as I had found in Argentinian Patagonia and many times I would cycle past a fellow bike traveller with only a nod or wave, without the excitement and conversation of meeting someone back down south. There were a lot of people on shorter tours, and they were having a great time, but the sense of community was lacking with people rushing to get to their next campsite rather than pausing to exchange information and tips.

While the views were terrific, the Carretera Austral felt more like a cycle touring holiday resort rather than the remote and barren land you read about in Chatwin, and I found myself exploring little and caring less. The bumpy roads started to annoy me as did the clouds of smoke which would be left as heavy trucks raced past me. People all camped in the same places, and it felt like I was on a bicycle conveyor belt with little interaction with the locals or even with other cycle tourists. I only had one memorable evening when I was cycling with a young Australian cyclist called Ellen, and we stopped in a field near Coyhaique to camp. We were joined by five Chilean hitchhikers, and we partied all night. There was loud rock music around a raging fire and we drank lots of cheap Chilean wine shouting "Patagonia sin represas!" which means 'Patagonia without dams', the slogan for the groups opposed to the building of hydro-electric dams in the region. The following morning I awoke hungover but knew I needed to leave the Carretera Austral to get my enjoyment and focus back. As I cycled out of town, I turned right to head back into Argentina and continue my trip away from the masses.

I was happy to be back on my own and looked forward to exploring a region I had no knowledge of. The road in Argentina was beautiful, and now the wind had mostly returned to manageable levels, I was able to cycle again at a normal pace and was averaging around 80 kilometres per day. As I cycled into the small town of Trevelin, I was blown away when I saw the street signs were written in both Spanish and Welsh. I could not believe it. I had stumbled across a small section of Patagonia which was founded by expatriate Welsh sheep farmers and the language and tradition of this place were all passed down from the original settlers. You could buy a Welsh cake or drink a Welsh beer and walk between the Welsh flags which were flying from many of the houses. It was so unexpected that I took a hostel so I could have a proper look around. I found out that the original settlers had come here to protect their native Welsh culture, which they felt was threatened by the English. The geography was similar to Wales, and they were able to farm and raise their livestock without problems. These settlers also brought the sport of rugby to the Argentinians, which they now excel at!

I was thrilled to leave the Carretera Austral since I was back into the more remote and quieter areas and felt like I was exploring again. I had stumbled across an area that otherwise I would have missed. Travelling by bike is beautiful in that sometimes you can come across a region that you never knew about. It may surprise you in its history or with a story of its people. It had been good to see lots of people cycling with the same passion for the outdoors, however, it felt like everyone was on their own little adventure rather than each person being part of something bigger. I often think that the round the world or long-distance community were individual spokes in a bigger wheel, with each person adding to the shared experience. I'd missed that community, and I was looking forward to once again finding my place in the wheel here in South America.

*Chapter Fourteen*

# HUMANITY

**M**y intention was originally to continue north, cross into Chile and head towards the capital city of Santiago. But since I was trying to avoid major cities, I changed course and headed towards the coastal town of Concepcion instead. This route would see me follow the sea once again, staying in Chile for another 1000 kilometres before crossing back into Argentina at the more remote mountain pass of San Francisco, standing at 5000 meters, which is where the high Andes Mountains act as the border between Chile and Argentina.

I reached Concepcion where I was due to spend the night with a WarmShowers host, but he was busy that evening, meaning I was unable to stay. I needed to scout a camp spot, and since it was getting dark, and as I was sitting in a park which had Wi-Fi, I thought I would camp there. Where I was sitting was busy, so I looked around for a quieter place. I followed a path that led uphill, pushing the bike up the steep hill in the fading sunlight. I was feeling a bit nervous since the park was quite public, but I thought that if I could find a place to hide, I would be alright for the night. I got to the top and put the bike down before walking a little way into the bush to see if there was a flat spot when I heard some people behind me. I jumped and quickly turned to see two men walking towards me. I was trapped on a ledge and felt quite nervous and defensive as I asked them what they wanted in broken Spanish. The light was fading and I felt exposed on the hilltop. The men backed off, giving me space to walk out. I relaxed slightly as it seemed they were not there to attack me as I grabbed my bike and started to push it back down the hill. The younger of the two men, with close-cut hair and wearing a smart blue jumper, spoke a little English and he told me it was not safe to camp here. He told me that there were lots of bandits around, and explained that they themselves were homosexual men who used this area for a little night-time fun. He then asked if I wanted to join in, to which I quickly said no and in my British way, thanked him for the offer before making my way quickly back down the hill. I felt a little apprehensive after my encounter and did not want to be followed, so I cycled out of town, quickly. I never did like camping in public spaces and prefer to find a more remote spot, since you are less likely to disturb or be disturbed by other people. This encounter was harmless, but could have been much worse had the men been wanting to rob me, as I was left exposed with nowhere to go. I needed to remember to stay safe and not put myself in potentially dangerous situations.

The following morning, I returned to Concepcion to grab some food and use the Wi-Fi again to contact my host who was now able to let me stay for two nights in his flat. It was that morning when I locked my bike up and went to the supermarket to use their toilet that my front pannier was robbed and I was fortunate to get everything back. Concepcion was turning out to be a frustrating place and my host Dan agreed that it could be dangerous since it is a large city, and that I had been lucky twice. I had a good time with Dan, and another cyclist who arrived from Colombia and travelled with a small Chihuahua called Diego. I had seen many cyclists with larger dogs in trailers, but this was my first time seeing a tiny Chihuahua, poking his head up from the handlebar bag. We all partied and drank homemade pisco sours, the traditional Chilean cocktail. It was a fun break from the bike and from the troubles in Concepcion, and it was a rest that I needed as I had not taken a break in around eight or nine days. I vowed to take better care of myself and be more careful when leaving the bike as I was more vulnerable than ordinary tourists. Everything I owned was on my bike and easily accessible from my panniers.

In Chile, although the cycling was good and I had beautiful mountain views, I was the loneliest I had ever been. Chilean Spanish is hard work because the locals speak very fast and with a lot of slang, so while my conversation was improving, it was very difficult for me to communicate. Even fluent Spanish speakers struggle here, so I had no chance. It was not just conversation I missed, I started to feel stuck in a rut of continually moving forward for the first time. Thoughts like *Why am I doing this when I have friends and family back home? Does anyone even care what I am trying to achieve? Do I even care anymore?* flowed through my mind.

Cycling on the Chilean coast became quite monotonous, and to overcome this and to counteract the loneliness, I started drinking a lot. I would often have a few beers at lunch followed by more beers or wine in the evening before I would pass out in my tent drunk, which was in itself quite dangerous, and did nothing to lift my mood or loneliness. I had reached a part of the cycle trip where everything had stagnated. I was not really enjoying myself anymore, but since I had this goal of reaching Reading, USA, I did not want to give up. I guess the truth was that I was not just lonely, I was becoming bored with the routine. It was the first time I had felt this way in two years and I needed a change.

Things started to get bad for me when I got to the town of La Serena, which is a beach party town 800 kilometres north of Valparaiso. I found a hostel which allowed camping but was about five kilometres away from the centre, which meant I had to cycle in to get my beers, wine and dinner. I decided to cheer myself up by making my favourite comfort food, spaghetti bolognese and listening to podcasts all evening. It was not that dissimilar to many previous nights, but the bolognese would be a real treat. I cooked a lovely meal and was feeling the buzz of the beers I had drunk, when I decided to go to town and party. I cycled back into town and by luck found a student bar area with lots of bars with different music genres. I walked into the first one, bought a one-litre bottle of beer and drank it at the bar. I ordered another which I couldn't finish, so left it and went dancing. I remember thinking I was like the classic WWE wrestler Kevin Nash who was the epitome of solo drinking and cool. The difference between him and me was that he was 6'10" with long hair and muscles while I am 5'11" with a shaved head, small arms and strong legs! I bar-hopped for a while before returning to the first bar, but by this time I was really drunk and most likely annoying everyone around me. I couldn't stand up straight, and I stumbled around the dance floor before battering into a couple of guys. It was accidental, but they didn't take it well and started shoving me around. I started pushing them back and before I knew it, I was on the floor looking up at five Chilean guys who all wanted me to get up and fight. I was too drunk to do anything and am pretty much a pacifist anyway, so I put my hands up to protest my innocence to the men who wanted to kick my head in. Luckily for me, the bouncer stepped in, separated us and threw me out of the bar, stopping them from following me out into the street.

I tried to get another beer in the bar opposite but was told firmly to go home. I staggered about before I found my bike, unlocked it, and cycled as fast as I could out of the bar area, with luckily nothing other than my ego bruised. I have no idea how I got home as I did not know the way and was very drunk, but I managed to get back to the campsite before crashing the bike on the soft sand, crawling into my tent and passing out. In the morning, I was a state and knew something had to change. My behaviour was getting me in trouble and I needed to curb my drinking. I was in a foreign country, getting into fights with people over nothing. This was not travelling; this was not even me. I booked another night in the campsite to recover from my hangover and did nothing but watch TV around the camp all day with a sore head and bad memories. I wrote in my diary that day that I needed to choose my life, my direction. I had control and needed to make the right choice. I knew adjustments had to be made, and in some ways, I had to hit rock bottom before I could start looking up again. I knew I was not ready to leave as I had so much to look forward to. Bolivia and Peru excited me as much as Honduras and El Salvador made me nervous. I was in a bad place, but the only way to overcome this was by cycling.

I decided I wanted to keep going and would push forward towards the mountains. My planned border crossing of San Francisco was about 500 kilometres ahead so I would aim for that and the town of Copiapo where I would stock up for the remote pass. I planned to hike to the peak which some say is the most accessible 6000-metre peak in the world as you start at 5000 metres, so no climbing gear is required. I decided to stop drinking and drank nothing other than Coke and water before getting to Copiapo. I stopped maybe 10 kilometres south of the town to camp in a nice little scrubland. I set up the tent before cycling down the road to buy an ice cream. As I left, it started to rain a little. I hadn't brought a coat to the shop, and soon I was in a full-on thunderstorm. The rain was hammering down like bullets, and the wind picked up to its previous Patagonian power. My tent was pegged out but without guide ropes and the door was left open when I returned, so everything inside was now soaked. I quickly zipped myself inside after putting out more pegs, and there I stayed for 12 hours as the storm howled around me. The rain was relentless and unexpected as this area of Chile typically sees very little rainfall. Here I was about to tackle the highest and most remote pass of the trip so far, and everything around me was falling down.

Once the storm had blown over, I popped into a tourist agency in Copiapo and they gave me the bad news. The roads and the pass were closed. The rain had caused flash flooding and major landslides which blocked roads and they had become too dangerous to cross. They were expecting more rain, all traffic was diverted, and they told me it would continue for another week, so I was unable to cross the border here. I was very disappointed not be able to cycle over the pass, although on reflection if I had been just one day faster, I would have been camping somewhere up on the mountain roads and would have been in severe danger of getting swept away, a predicament more dangerous than getting into a little scuffle in a Chilean bar. Perhaps getting drunk was not such a bad thing after all as it had delayed my progress by a day. It is funny how things can work out for the best. I had no choice but to change my plans and rather than cycle back to Argentina, I decided I would stay in Chile and head north up the Atacama Desert.

The Atacama is the driest non-polar desert on the planet and crossing by bike would make for a tough and different challenge. Water would again be my priority, just like in Australia, as it was going to be hot and barren. Also, I would be slow as the road was not only remote, but rose to the height of 2700m on a slow incline. I wanted to be in the mountains, but it was the desert which was calling again. The universe had spoken.

Before I had reached the desert road, I had heard from my family that my grandad was ill and had been in the hospital for a few days with chest problems. My grandad, one of the calmest and kindest men I had ever met, had been with me on this trip before, in spirit, when I went to Kluang in Malaysia to visit his former WWII station. It made me sad to see pictures of how skinny he looked, and he looked like he was losing the battle with his lungs. My parents told me he was proud of me and was always asking about where in the world I was. I was saddened to hear that he was unwell, but it was not altogether unexpected since he was over 80 at this time.

I had just got to the town of Tortel on the coast, and I sat down next to a tourist information office to get Wi-Fi, and my phone started going off with all the messages from the family. A message from my sister asking me to call home and another from my parents telling me to call. I was nervous as deep down I knew what had happened. I called home to hear the news that my grandad had passed away suddenly in his sleep during the evening of the 19th April 2017. I was so upset. I called my sister who was also upset, and I didn't know what to do. I was thousands of miles from home and alone outside a random tourist office with nobody to talk to or share in my grief. Unable to speak the local language and share my pain, I sat on that step in the tourist office and cried, and that moment was the loneliest and saddest I had been on the entire trip. I wished my family were here with me, but they were at home, grieving themselves, but together. I did the only thing I knew to do and found a hotel room for the night, bought some beers, and drank them in my hotel room thinking of my granddad, who was a keen beer drinker himself. With every beer, I toasted my grandad and missed him and hoped he would have been proud of me. I paid him my respects that night and somehow knew that he was happy for me to celebrate his life in this way.

In the morning when I spoke with my mum, she told me that his wish was that if anything happened to him, I was not to return home for the funeral but stay on the road. His time had passed, and he did not want me to fly home because I might not come back and finish the trip. He was right: although I missed him terribly and not going to the funeral would be difficult, mostly as I wanted to be there for my mum, I chose to continue. I turned down the kind offer from my sister to pay for my flights home and stayed in contact with my parents in case they wanted me there, but we all knew nothing would bring him back. This was hard, but this also gave me the motivation to continue. I looked to the stars and decided that I was going to continue this trip for him, my Grandad. I was not going to stop for anything and I would finish it to make him proud. So, with a heavy heart and a huge sense of loss, I pushed my bike off into the Atacama Desert, heading north.

Battling through the Atacama Desert was a lesson in perseverance. The road rises slowly at around 5% gradient from sea level to 2700 metres for over 600 kilometres, and everywhere you look you see the arid desert on both sides. The landscape was as bleak as my mood, and I wanted to cycle north, away from Taltal, to be able to forget and remember all at the same time. The only way to go was forward. It was similar to cycling in the outback of Australia, but here there were more cars, fewer services and much less wildlife. The only way to make progress was just to get up each day and cycle as far as the daylight would let me.

The first night I pushed my bike through the heavy sand towards a derelict building. I was pushing into the wind which howled with a ferocity over the empty plain, as the wheels of the bike slowly sank into the soft sand. It was like pushing through jelly. As I got close to the structure, I realised it was a train line and what looked like an abandoned station building. *This must have been how they built the road*, I mused before setting up my bed for the night. I made a small fire, cooked some dinner and looked up at the millions and millions of stars overhead. With nothing around me, there was no light pollution, and I could see the Milky Way above me, shining in all its beauty. There was something in the air that night. Even though I was totally alone that night in the desert, I felt a presence with me, as if my Grandad was checking on me. I felt like he was making sure I was OK and, in his happy, go-lucky way, telling me that I was on the right track and everything was going to be alright. I slept in complete silence until around 2 a.m. when a goods train came thundering past with lights on full beam and horn blowing for some unknown reason, waking me with a start!

As I continued north, the wind started to pick up and occasionally a sand storm would blow through, making me reach into my bags for my scarf to cover my face and protect my eyes from the sharp sand whipping across the road. The lack of supplies would have also been a problem, but the verge was lined with the shrines for people who have died in car crashes on the road. The sheer number of shines speaks to the danger of travelling this road. They often had several big bottles of drinking water next to them, so the spirits would never go thirsty in the desert. I would stop by one and take a little water: I was sure the person or family would not mind that their shrine was helping another traveller on their way. I know I would be happy for my spirit to help others in need. On a few occasions, I would see a shrine that was so ornate that it would be closed off with a sliding door, enabling me to take shelter from the wind and sleep inside. This always made me a bit nervous, not because of the spirits, but in case the family turned up wanting to pay their respects and there was a gringo sleeping on the floor. I am not sure how they would have reacted, but I never encountered any problems.

As I left that morning, I began cycling at my slow and steady pace, but my head space was filled with a new and annoying companion. At each turn of the pedal, there would be a loud and audible click. At first, this did not bother me, but as it continued, it began to grow more and more frustrating. I tried to apply grease and oil to the pedals, but this didn't work and I realised that I must have some grit inside my bottom bracket, the device which holds the cranks to the bicycle. I did not have the specialist tool required to fix this problem, so there was nothing I could do to stop the noise. Each turn of the pedals brought its own little irritation. I even found myself stopping and shouting at my bike as if that would fix it. I solved the situation in the short term by listening to music, but I knew my batteries soon would be exhausted and I would have to endure the mild torture of the rhythmic clicking.

I was close to the plateau so the uphill cycling had become easier, and I was able to make a slightly faster pace. Although the sound of the grit inside my bearing was increasingly annoying, the sheer fact that I was going faster made my mood improve. I was not fast, but I was steady, and a steady cyclist is a happy cyclist. I was going strong until midday, where my belly started to complain of hunger. All I had to eat for lunch was plain spaghetti or plain oats, so it was not with any real excitement that I started to look for somewhere out of the wind to cook my food. When presented with a choice of two simple carbs, the joy of stopping is replaced with a feeling of resentment and disappointment. It was not long until I saw a building on the side of the road and aimed for this for my spaghetti lunch.

As I pulled closer, the building looked to be in better condition than I first thought, clean white walls, large windows, and even an electricity port on the outside. I immediately saw the potential to charge my phone and therefore drown out the noise my pedals were making.

As I stepped off the bike, I saw a police vehicle parked behind the building, meaning someone was in. I approached cautiously, and a young Chilean police guard came out and greeted me, asking what I wanted. He was a small man in uniform, but he did not look happy to see me, a contrast to the excited greetings from my previous meetings with the Chilean police. I told him about my bike trip, about my need for somewhere to stop for lunch and asked if I was able to charge my phone. He looked disapprovingly at me at first and told me to go. In broken Spanish, I begged for a few minutes shelter from the sun and wind, and he eventually relented, giving me a precious five minutes before he wanted me gone. I was downhearted by the experience, so I sat in the shade with my phone collecting power from the external plug socket. I was tired but happy just to sit. I wanted to try to maximise my time for rest, so I didn't bother to eat anything. I just sat there.

After five minutes, the young guard came out, his stony face set. I started to gather my bits together, but he motioned me to stay where I was, and pulled an ice-cold bottle of water out from the inside of his jacket. I grinned my thanks. He could obviously see that I was no threat at all, I was just a lonely cyclist resting in the shade of his outbuilding. We talked briefly before he told me he had to go back inside.

Slowly I drank the ice-cool water and felt my body rehydrating. I had been drinking warm and tepid water for the previous six days, so this refreshed my body like nothing else. A coolness which infused my insides with icy joy, it cooled me down instantly, and my mouth was thankful for this simple gift. I had been sitting in the shade for about 15 minutes now when the guard came out of his air-conditioned building a third time. This time he had a smile across his face. He was holding a small bag and he offered it to me, telling me to take it. I looked down inside the bag to see a treasure trove of delicious food. He had given me what could only have been his lunch: a cheese sandwich, a cereal bar, yoghurt and an apple. I protested, but he quickly shut me down telling me he was off shift in an hour and would go to the restaurant in his home town 60 kilometres away. My spirit lifted. My mood lifted. My heart ached for the kindness of humanity, and my stomach churned in the expectant joy of this varied and delicious food. Everything I had been feeling and struggling with suddenly eased as I took the first bite into the most amazing cheese sandwich I had ever eaten. Not only had my palate been starved of taste in the desert, but my soul had been starved of compassion. The loneliness, isolation and all the depressive thought processes started to lift. The young Chilean guard never knew how happy I was to sit there and eat. It was as if I was in a computer game, and my character had just received a power-up. I sat outside the house for half an hour before leaving and felt more refreshed and energised than when I first started cycling in South America. I knocked on his door and thanked the young man with all my heart, he gave me another bottle of water and wished me luck.

As I pedalled away, I felt the joy of a shared connection. It felt like happiness was radiating through my body. I had not spoken to a single person for six days and had been struggling with thoughts of self-doubt. Deep inside my chest, I felt a nagging pull to return home and be with my loved ones to grieve and reminisce. But now, as I cycled away, I was smiling. I knew I was on the right path. To experience pure joy, one must feel sadness first. Every time I think of that part of the trip, I think of the kindness of the young guard rather than all the times I struggled through the desert.

I put in my headphones and was able to listen to a podcast rather than the annoying noise. I knew that I could get the bike fixed the following day. I continued cycling, my eyes wandering around the expansive desert valley around me, an alien planet of rock and dust. I knew how lucky I was to be out here and to be dwarfed by everything around me.

I thought of my Grandad who did not want me to return home for his funeral. He knew I was living a life very few would ever understand. I believe he was able to understand me: he had wanted to see the world as a young man, as had I. I was seeing it for myself now, and would always think of this trip as something which would bond his memory to mine. I wanted to finish this bike ride for us both, and I felt reinvigorated after experiencing the beauty of humanity simply served up in a cheese sandwich.

*Chapter Fifteen*
# FRIENDS

After the silence of the desert, when I reached the tourist town of San Pedro de Atacama, it was no surprise that I was unable to keep quiet. I checked into a little hostel in the centre and proceeded to talk the ear off of everyone around me. It was quite cathartic, and I made friends quickly. San Pedro sits in the middle of Northern Chile and is surrounded by craters, geysers and hot springs. It looks more like Mars than Chile due to all the red, jagged rock formations surrounding you. The remoteness combined with the striking landscape also meant it was quite expensive and touristy, so after just two days of exploring I was ready to jump back on the bike and head into Bolivia.

My original plan was to get my Bolivian visa in San Pedro before cycling straight up 1500 metres and reaching the famous Lagunas route of Southern Bolivia. In this isolated and surreal landscape, you cycle past flamingos and bright pink lakes. I was prepared and ready having read and printed out some useful guide information from the helpful

*Pikes on Bikes* website, but just like the high passes in Chile, the weather stopped me in my tracks.

An unexpected storm brought heavy snowfall over the pass, making the border impassable, and all travel was stopped including heavy goods traffic. The authorities told me that the border would be closed for a week minimum, and they were not giving out visas in an effort to stop intrepid travellers from attempting to cross. Down-hearted, I had two options; to either wait in San Pedro for a week until the road became safe, or to backtrack and try to cross at the western border at Ollague. I checked again with the immigration in the morning, but since it had snowed again, there would be no movement possible for at least seven days. As I was not very good at sitting still, I decided to cycle back 100 kilometres to Calama, where I would stay at a hostel before climbing up to Ollague. This would mean skipping the Lagunas route, but would save time and money and enable me to keep moving. I was happy with my decision and started to head back the way I had come. It took me two days to reach Calama where I checked into the cheapest hostel in town at around midday.

As I entered the hostel, I was greeted by three other cyclists who were there resting. I met Israel, a solo cyclist from Brazil and Ellen and Pim, a couple from Holland. They were all travelling north, and I was happy to report to them that the pass should be open by the time they arrived in San Pedro.

I always found a real and immediate connection with other cyclists who have travelled the same road. We shared stories of the people we had met and of the road we had all cycled. After feeling so alone at times in Chile, it was great to share this evening with fellow cyclists who really understood what it is like to cycle long distances. I left alone the following morning, but we all swapped phone numbers, and with the slow mountain roads ahead, I was sure we would meet again. The road up to Ollague was on a steady incline, and soon I was above 3000 metres and climbing higher. The mountains of the Andes were starting to show off their beauty, and I felt confident. Luckily, I did not feel the full effect of altitude sickness. For some reason each time I would climb above 3000 metres, I would receive a short bout of diarrhoea just for 12 hours or so, before feeling fine the following morning, and would not require any additional medicine or acclimatisation.

The Bolivian border is nothing more than just a few huts, standing proud between the wire fence in the barren landscape. I was quickly processed by the guards, as I popped my head and passport into each shed and signed the necessary paperwork. I camped that night just a few kilometres away from the border, and the desolation and emptiness of Bolivia quickly became apparent. The road was a series of marked yellow and brown tracks. There was nothing on either side except mountains raising their colossal heads up from the ground. I camped behind some rocks to escape the howling wind, and I smiled to myself, happy to be here. Bolivia marked a new start and a new stage of South America with wilder landscapes, a real sense of adventure and an easier more traditional language.

My first goal was to cycle to Uyuni and ride across the famous salt desert, where hexagonal mirrored salt spans 100 kilometres square. I figured it would take me about three days to get there. I had enough reserves but purchased some extra snacks and quinoa in advance just in case, and I set off towards the salt flats. The tracks I was following were unmarked, so I navigated mainly using my phone to confirm my position, pleased that I was on the right track, both in terms of navigation and my mental state. I continued until I found an abandoned salt mine. I was sure it was abandoned since the door was hanging off and the windows were smashed and thought this would make a perfect home for the night. I cycled up and pushed my bike inside. The office still had scribblings on the whiteboard and paper on the desk, but since it was all dated from 2009, I was sure I would be undisturbed. Looking around, I also found a small sink and was surprised to see the water working. Happy with my campsite, I made up my bed and rested.

I slept well, awoke, made my morning oats and packed everything away, ready to leave. I then remembered the tap and filled up my water bottles for filtering later and brushed my teeth. I did not filter the water when brushing and thought I would be OK. I even drank a little bit, thinking I would be fine as my guts were pretty resilient at this point. I didn't think anything more of it as I followed the salty sand trails towards Uyuni, but in the afternoon I started to feel unwell and had very little energy. I was a bit worried as I was about 60 kilometres from the nearest town on rough roads but managed to find a small waterhole next to some rocks and decided this would be the safest place to rest, so I stopped and set up camp.

I could not eat anything, and that night I could not sleep as my stomach was rumbling. I had to keep burping to let the gas out, and it smelt like rotten eggs. I knew I was in trouble, but being so remote there was nothing to do but wait out the sickness. I had water sickness before in Central Asia, so I knew it was a waiting game. I stayed in my tent in the middle of nowhere for three days, only leaving it to run outside to go to the toilet behind the rocks or to filter some water to drink. My only food reserves were nuts, bread and avocado but this only made me feel worse, so I pretty much starved myself, unable to keep anything down. On the second day, I began to get a little worried. I knew if I had caught something serious, then there was no way I would be able to get help in such a remote area. There had not been a passing car in two days, although my only real break from the tent was to rush into the rocky scrubland behind me. The sickness would come in waves so I would begin to feel better, and start to think about getting back on the road before it all came crashing down around me again with sulphuric burps and more diarrhoea.

On the third day, I awoke and was starving. This was a good sign as it meant that I was able to eat for the first time in three days. I ate all my remaining dry food of bread and nuts and I could feel my body getting its strength back. I was relieved that I would finally be able to leave the tent. By midday, as I had not had any recurring bouts of sickness, I packed up and slowly cycled away from the waterhole knowing that I could never unsee the mess I'd left behind the rocky scrubland! I was on the mend though, and managed to cycle about 30 kilometres that day before stopping and sleeping a long deep sleep.

I awoke the next morning feeling better. Although I could not shake the sulphuric burps, I was able to cycle and decided the best medicine was to keep moving, I followed my compass and GPS across the salt tracks headed towards the Salar. I stopped about 10 kilometres from the salt desert and rested the night before taking on the beautiful salt wilderness. The water sickness would later be diagnosed as Guardia Fever, and is usually treated with a course of antibiotics. Since I was in the middle of nowhere my 'wait it out' technique did the job, and I was back on the bike and cycling again with memories of the sickness soon behind me.

I was excited to finally reach the Salar. I was cycling into the world's biggest salt desert with salt crystals crunching under my heavy tyres. It was as beautiful as the pictures made out, with the large flat salt pan spanning the horizon in every direction. I could cycle in any direction I wanted, there was nobody else around, and it felt like total freedom. Just being here was good for the soul and all thoughts of getting sick were put to the back of my mind as I shed all my clothes and took to riding naked in the middle of the salt, in what has become a touring cyclist tradition. There was no one around as far as the eye could see, so I was perfectly happy to cycle naked as I knew I would not give anyone a shock! I cycled about 3 kilometres naked, taking a few pictures before the cold started to take effect and I decided it would be better for everyone concerned to get dressed again.

In the middle of the Salar is an island called Isla Incahuasi, where a small museum shares the space with towering 4 metre high cacti. I stopped to look around and took some photos and got chatting to the people who ran it. They told me cyclists often take a room here, and they had a classroom attached to the museum where I could sleep, where it would not get too cold. It was forecast to be -15 that night, so I took them up on their offer and was introduced to two backpackers also staying the night. It was indeed warmer in the classroom, and we all bedded down on the mattresses provided and watched the star show through the large window which overlooked the open sky.

Cycling the Salar was beautiful, and as I got closer to the town of Uyuni, I took pictures of the field of flags, and the Dakar Rally statue, all with my bike displayed proudly in the foreground. It was a place of magnificent beauty with bright blue skies giving way at the horizon to flat white salt. Sunglasses were essential as the salt reflects the sunlight right into your eyes. The sense of scale is magnified by the vast flat ground. I could see a hundred kilometres in every direction and not see another person, and I loved it. Who needs company when you have the most amazing views, made all the more remarkable as you are travelling there by your own power. When I reached the township of Uyuni, I took a hostel for two days to recover and to wash the bike.

The salt covered everything, and I needed to give the bike a good wash as I didn't want the salt to corrode the steel frame. Once washed and rested, I was able to take the mountain ride towards Potosi and then Sucre.

Cycling in this region of the Andes was fantastic, especially the ride from Uyuni to Potosi as you are always either going up or down, never on the flat, and the stunning views were worth the effort required. You climb higher and higher before looking back down and marvelling at both your progress and the views. The highest point of the road is 4400 metres, which takes some effort due to the thin air, but after climbing solidly for two days, you are rewarded with a whole day of downhill riding: back and forth you meander down the roads, past fading mountains and little shops and businesses. As you get lower, the vegetation starts to appear again with the reds and greens replacing yellow and white. As you get to the bottom of the valley, you are in a cactus field with tall plants waving hello as you cycle happily past. I met another cyclist in Potosi who told me she cried as she cycled this route and I understood why as it is surprisingly special. It was a real joy to find moments of pure beauty like these, to stumble upon such a fun and varied downhill which lasts in my memory much longer than any thoughts of times of stress or hardship.

My arrival in Sucre was greeted by white Spanish style buildings set around a well-kept central plaza with little street vendors dotted around and people all relaxing on benches in the shade of large trees. It was pleasant, almost Mediterranean and you could see the Spanish style in all the buildings around you. Sucre shares the title of capital city of Bolivia with La Paz and is the administrative centre. It is much quieter and peaceful compared to the industrial capital in the north.

I had planned to stop here for two weeks since it was the perfect place to relax and learn Spanish. I had booked a hostel called the Celtic Cross in the north of the city which conducted its own Spanish lessons and gave a discount on the rooms if you took the classes. It was a picturesque courtyard-style hostel filled with friendly and welcoming travellers and made my stay here memorable. I really loved Sucre, you could go out for a two-course dinner for less than three dollars, and it really had a European feel to the city with coffee shops and little artisan bakeries on the street corners. My decision to learn Spanish in Bolivia was made for two reasons. It was cheaper there than in Chile or Argentina, and it was also closer to the Spanish spoken in the rest of South and Central America. The lessons worked out at five dollars per hour, and I booked lessons in blocks of four hours. This was an intensive course, but meant that I could learn quickly and build upon the words I had learnt with rules and grammar. My teacher was a beautiful young Bolivian lady, (which was more than a little distracting at times!), but she was a great teacher, and I learnt a lot over the two weeks. I was not perfect, but it gave me something to build on and would enable me to be more confident when speaking with the locals.

I enjoyed my 32nd birthday in Sucre with a young English backpacker named Nikita. We partied the night away in an Irish/Bolivian bar drinking shots until 4 a.m. We danced and partied with the locals and I practiced my newly learned Spanish with the local señoritas. Unfortunately, I kept calling them 'hermoso' rather than 'hermosa' which is like calling someone handsome rather than beautiful! Sucre is one of the places on my travels that I would return to in a heartbeat and is my favourite city in the whole of South America. It is somewhere I feel would be entirely liveable. While in Sucre I got a text from Israel, the cyclist from Brazil I had met in Chile. He was meeting some cyclists in a bar in the centre of town, and I went to join them.

I was reunited with Israel, Pim and Ellen and also introduced to Kenneth and Marie from Denmark. It was a meeting of kindred spirits, and we ate, drank and laughed together till late into the evening. We were all staying in town and would meet a few times while we were there. We all became firm friends and made an effort to keep in touch and share information on the road ahead as we were all headed North.

After two weeks of rest, and with my Spanish tongue starting to take root, it was time to leave. My intention was to head towards Cochabamba, a large market city before taking the jungle road towards La Paz, which would be both more beautiful and exciting than the straight and more direct highway. I was cycling up a small hill when I heard a bang and my rear wheel stopped. Worried, I quickly hopped off the bike to see my rear dérailleur had somehow got twisted up in the rear wheel, I had snapped two spokes, and my dérailleur hanger was bent. Unable to cycle, I made a field repair to limp to the next village. I was only able to cycle in one gear, but the village was only five kilometres away so with some pushing up the hills, I made it with no real issues.

Upon arrival at the village, the bike shop did not have the replacement hanger which I needed, so with my bike unrideable, I jumped on a bus to Cochabamba where I knew there were several bike shops dotted around. The bus ticket was cheap, and they tied the bike to the roof. It was a bumpy and twisty four-hour ride to the city. I arrived just before midnight, but there were still a lot of people around, and I took the first hostel I saw, which also turned out to be a brothel, but it was cheap, so I didn't mind.

The following day, I took my bike to a decent bike shop and luckily they had the part I needed. I also got them to put on a new bottom bracket and front crank. This, however, proved to be a big error as the only front crank they had was designed more for city touring than long-distance, but I cycled off happy, and it was not until the first day when I was trying to climb the challenging hills on the jungle route that I realised something was wrong. The roads were steep and all made of cobbles, and I was having a tough time getting traction on the back wheel, as the gearing was now too big. I struggled and sweated for four hours before sitting down tired and exhausted. I was moving about three kilometres per hour, and it would have been faster to walk. This road had got the better of me, and I was getting fed up and with such slow progress. I knew I didn't have enough supplies to make it to the first mapped town. Defeated and dejected, I turned around, knowing it was the safer thing to do and bumped back down on the cobblestones, which was just as tricky as travelling up. I was fit, but I didn't realise the effect that gearing can have on the bike, and this was my first lesson in that department. Unable to ride the steep jungle roads, I decided to head straight for La Paz on the highway where I would stay at the Casa de Ciclista which has a large workshop on the ground floor. Here, with the help of the owner, Christian, I would be able to fit a more comfortable gear for little money. It was a shame not to travel the jungle road as it would have been exciting, but to continue would have been both no fun and likely dangerous if I had run out of water. On trips like these, you are always learning and with experience comes more knowledge.

As I took the highway, I was cresting a small climb and saw some shops and coffee shops where I decided to have a rest and grab a drink. I saw two people rise up from their chairs, shout "Tim" and run over to me. I didn't recognise them at first but quickly saw it was both Kenneth and Marie. It was a warm reunion with my two friends, and we hugged on the top of the hill before sitting for coffee. We agreed to cycle to La Paz together, and it was great to cycle with like-minded folk and be able to talk and enjoy the views and lunches together. We would often stop for cheap food in the restaurants or eat cheese sandwiches overlooking mountain vistas. For five days we rode together, camping out in beautiful locations and sleeping the sleep of the weary cyclist.

I enjoyed cycling with them, but unfortunately, Kenneth got sick as we neared La Paz. He was struck by the same virus I had suffered from in the South and had the same sulphuric burps and yellow poop. He needed rest, so they took a hostel and a bus to La Paz whereas I carried on. The sickness gets everyone at some point and with my sympathy, I wished him the best, and we parted at Calamarca before agreeing to meet again in La Paz.

As I entered La Paz, I was greeted with lots and lots of traffic. I got my first glimpse of the city, one of the highest in the world, as I descended from 4500 metres and I saw millions of houses in the valley below. It looked as though I was gazing down onto a model city. The road became busy with passing cars and trucks blowing their exhaust in my face as I descended 500 metres down to the heart of the city. It was not for the faint-hearted as the road had so much traffic. I was super confident at this point but still took my time, with my helmet on, taking the descent slowly and safely. I arrived into the centre of La Paz and cycled right up to the Casa de Ciclista and knocked on the door before being greeted by a friendly face. "Israel!" I shouted and gave him a big hug before he helped me lug my bike and luggage up the stairs.

I stayed here for four days as we made plans and fixed our bikes. I was able to purchase a new gearing from Christian, the owner, and I put on a super low 'granny gear' to compensate for my troubles. I would have no further problems over the mountains. Christian ran the casa from afar, and did not stay here himself. He was the kind of person who likes everything in its place. It was really kind of him to allow so many people to stay in his apartment when it must have frustrated him to see bikes and luggage dotted around all over the place. When it came to being a bike mechanic, he was second to none and helped me set up the new cranks and gearing. I learnt a lot from him, although we had to spend an hour looking for a tool which was not put back in the right place.

The Casa in La Paz is located right in the centre of the city which makes it a magnet for cycle tourists. There were six to eight people all staying which makes for a perfect mix when you are chatting around the coffee table during the evenings. Planning routes and fixing my bike was the main reason for me to be in La Paz since for me, the city was otherwise too busy and crowded. It was here I first met Greg and Morgane, a good looking young French couple with positive attitudes who I would depart from La Paz with.

After being in La Paz for four days we left the city. Rather than cycle back up the busy and steep mountain road, we all loaded our bikes into the cable cars which would take us out of the city. Getting our bikes onto the sky lift was a real hassle as the guards at the station would not allow us to take our bikes in the lifts, so we had to carry them up the stairs and over the barriers which made a simple job much more difficult. But at least their lifts didn't get dirty!

I rode with my new French friends for two days towards Lake Titicaca until our roads split, and I headed to the southern town of Copacabana, while they headed around the north side of the lake. Lake Titicaca was a real beauty with blue waters stretching across my view until they reached the edge of the horizon. I arrived at Copacabana and checked into a hostel before sitting down to eat a big bag of giant popcorn I had just bought, when I heard a knock at my door. I opened it and was warmly greeted by a delighted Marie, saying hello. They had checked into the same hostel and seen my bike so asked the owner for my room number. It was great to see them again, and we went out for a final Bolivian dinner that night before agreeing to cycle together over the border and into Peru. It was great having so many friends to cycle with, and it seemed I was continually bumping into people I knew. We used our time that evening to plan the next stage of our trips and get ready for the real ups and downs of Peru.

*Chapter Sixteen*

# PACHAMAMA

**P**eru is the spine of the Andes and where the most prominent peaks are found; therefore, the road is a constant battle between uphill and downhill. There are also three routes to take: the busy and flat coastal highway, the hilly but beautiful mountain route or the fun and exciting jungle road. I wanted to encompass all three roads in my time here and planned to take the mountains until Cusco, before heading to the jungle for a while, then cycle over the Andes once again to reach the coast and the border with Ecuador. With all our plans made, we left the town of Juliaca as a group of five, having met up again with Greg and Morgane, and our little gang cycled north, taking in the sights, sounds, and culinary delights of Peru.

The one highlight we all wanted to see was the rainbow mountain in Peru, which sits 100 kilometres south of Cusco. I'd not heard about the mountain until our host in Juliaca showed me a picture of the beautiful colourful layers of rock, and just like the Perito Moreno Glacier in Argentina, I knew I had to see this incredible natural feature. Drawn as always to nature, this for me became the focal point of my journey in Southern Peru and something which excited me more than the famous ruins at Machu Picchu. The road rose and fell, but time flew as we talked and joked on the inclines and sped down the descents. As we arrived into the town of Pitumarca, an authentic Latin American fiesta was under-way. Local people in their traditional clothes of bright red jackets and hats were all dancing around the central square of this little town. Beer was passed around as the music played, and everyone cheered and laughed. In Peru, it is common when you are handed the shared bottle of beer and plastic cup to pour a little bit onto the ground first. This is for Pachamama (mother earth) and is a tradition which invites the planet to the party and a concept which I really liked. We partied on the streets that night, drinking beer and chicha, which is a beer made from corn. Kenneth and Greg went to look for our host as unfortunately, we did not have a phone number for him, so did not know where he lived. They spoke the best Spanish, and tried asking around the locals. It was not long before he was found and we left the party to meet him and wash before rejoining the festivities.

We all stayed in his spare room, and it was pretty cosy with all five of us sleeping on the floor next to each other, but it was warm and safe, and we were happy to sleep anywhere after being on the road for so long. Kenneth and Marie were going to go on a separate trip to Ausangate Mountain on their fat bikes, leaving me to visit the rainbow mountain with Greg and Morgane.

It was a beautiful quiet road up the mountain and we cycled uphill for two days to reach the start of the hike which would take us to the top of the mountain. With a stream on our right and trees giving way to views of little villages, it was a fantastic ride. When we stopped to camp in a school after our first day, we even had time to play football with the local villagers. After running around for five minutes Greg and I quickly started to play in goal, as at 4000 metres, we did not have the lungs to compete with the kids who lived at this altitude all year round. We arrived at the top the following day around midday, paid our five dollars and went in to find all the tourists leaving the summit. Rainbow Mountain can attract hundreds of tourists each day from Cusco, so we got lucky with the timing. As we made the final steps up to 5200 metres and onto the viewpoint, we were the only ones there. We danced and hugged and gazed in wonder at the beautiful nature in front of us. It was even more stunning than the pictures. Light reflected off the coloured rocks in a special moment shared with friends who were also giddy on nature and the lack of oxygen. I wonder if mass tourism will lead to a decline in the beauty of the area. We counted ourselves lucky we were able to visit this as we were passing through. It was the perfect stop before getting to Cusco and reaching the tourist centre of Peru.

Cusco is famous for being the gateway to Machu Picchu and at the hostel, everyone was either talking about their trips having just come from the renowned temple or was in a discussion about how to get there. Everyone but me. While travelling, I had started to understand my likes and dislikes, and had come to the realisation that I did not enjoy visiting old historical monuments, which also often had high entry costs. So I made the decision not to visit this most famous of places. Machu Picchu would have cost me over $100, and I knew I could cycle around Peru for twenty days with that amount of money. Although I am sure the hike to the top is beautiful, I did not want to pay for the privilege when I had already experienced the beautiful trek to Rainbow Mountain. Part of this decision came down to my limited budget. When you are low on funds, you have to save your money for things you really want to do. I had about £1800 left with eleven months remaining so needed to ensure I made it last.

I stayed in Cusco for four days, in a hostel called Estrellita which is recommended by cyclists and overlanders as it is cheap, has plenty of space and is right next to a French bakery, so breakfast croissants became a welcome tradition, especially for my French friends! I left Cusco alone, with my friends either going to Machu Picchu or headed to the coast. I had a great time, but it was time to get back on the road alone. The great thing about South America is that thanks to the network of Casas and there being a typical route that cyclists follow, it would not be long until we saw each other again. The northern road is challenging as you climb towards Huancayo with the road rising up the mountain to over 4000 metres, then falling back to 2000 metres before climbing up again. The change in scenery and agriculture is so different between the two altitudes, with scrubland and cold winds at the top of the passes, but warm weather and mango trees on the bottom. The lowland also saw me getting attacked by sand flies every night. I would have to sit in the mesh in my tent to prevent me from getting bitten. The sand fly bites itched for a few days and would be most noticeable and annoying right before going to bed, so I tried to avoid getting bitten at all times.

While the elevation made the cycling tough, thankfully the mountain slopes of Peru were gentle, and the inclines steady. I would just put the bike in its lowest gear and turn the pedals over and over, and I found I could cycle around 40 kilometres and climb 2000m of elevation in a day. I put some music on and occasionally stopped to look down or out over the views. The roads in Peru are all around a 5% gradient, so while you can gain lots of elevation in a day, it is actually quite comfortable cycling. As a result, you do not need to get off and push. This is a marked difference to places like Ecuador or Guatemala where the gradients are 10–15%, and although the passes there are not as high, it is much more challenging work with a fully laden bike

By this time I had reached Huancayo and rather than going straight and taking the direct route to Huaraz and the Cordillera Blanca region, I planned to head east and towards the jungle for warmer temperatures and something new to see. I turned east at Huancayo and with the road starting at 3000 metres, I thought it would be all downhill from there, but I did not account for the two hidden passes before the big descent. The beauty of not having a real map made this route a pleasant, but tough surprise with some great camping at the lake at the top of the pass at 4500 metres. Finally, the road took me down to the jungle, and it was a beautiful ride. I had to descend through the clouds, which sounds romantic but is actually very cold, wet and slightly dangerous since the water vapour steamed up my glasses and I couldn't see anything.

Clear of the cloud line, I cycled into a new and colourful world with brightly coloured wooden houses lining the roads beside palm trees and streams. It was stunning and warm, and the people would shout and wave as I went past. I stayed in an empty wooden barn just before reaching the town of Satipo and that morning, I went to buy some bananas for breakfast, 10 for a dollar. Fresh fruit like mango and papaya also hung from trees, waiting to be picked, so my stomach was happy to be somewhere new and eating the good stuff I could not get in the mountains.

The jungle was much more populous than I expected with lots of small villages dotted along the roadside. I saw monkeys, snakes, lizards and spiders. I often camped in the land between the villages or on the football field in the village. The people were all welcoming and hospitable apart from one village. I stopped and asked two local ladies if I could camp, and they pointed to the football field and said "OK, two other cyclists also stopped here a few nights ago". I took this as a good omen and to show respect I camped at the far end of the field, away from people's houses. I set up my camp, cooked and ate my dinner, and it was just starting to get dark when across the field came a group of men. It must have been all the men in the village, and each one held a bright torch as they made their way to my tent. They looked angry and on a mission as I stepped outside and told them my intention. This village was not your average Peruvian village; it was actually an indigenous community, and they spoke their own language and had their own traditions. They were upset I had not asked the chief, and in recognising the problem, I turned to the eldest man, who was in the centre of the group, apologised in Spanish and English and told him that I would only be one night and would be no trouble. The torches burned the back of my eyes, and I was worried this could turn into a serious situation.

I explained to the chief that I would leave in the morning, but he told me he was worried I would impregnate the women of the village. I reassured him that this was not my intention – I was just a cyclist, a tourist – and this seemed to calm them all down. I wondered if this was a fear borne out of reality – had a gringo previously been through this community and impregnated all their women or was it just a story? But I did not want to offend and told them I would sleep now and leave first thing in the morning. This seemed to placate the menfolk, and they left me alone to my tent.

Relieved and amused by the situation, I didn't sleep well that night and as I woke up early in the morning to the sounds of the village cockerel I decided to make a swift exit. The chief of the village then came over to me and asked for money. I gave him two dollars as a token, but this did not seem to suffice, he wanted twenty. I told him this was too much and would be unable to give him any more. I did not want to be rude, but all I had done was camp in a field. He thought he was in the right since I was a tourist. While I did not mind giving something to the community, his persistence at asking for twenty felt too much. I quickly packed up, and I left him there with his two dollars. It was an interesting experience, one that led to fear and uncertainty on both sides. I did not want to put myself or a local indigenous community in that place again. I wondered if the lady who permitted me to camp in the field knew what would happen, or if two other cyclists ever did pass as the reaction from the men made it feel that camping on the field was not a normal thing that happened.

The road became dusty before quickly turning to mud: a thick wet brown sludge caused by heavy rain and continuous roadworks. The Peruvian government was upgrading the road network, and a large part of the road was dug up. I had to stop cycling as the mud would roll up the wheels and get stuck between the brake blocks and the front forks. I only had a small clearance between my wheel and forks, so even a small amount of this sticky mud would quickly collect and stop the wheels from moving. I was always on the lookout for a trusty stick, and I would often be on the roadside using it to clear out the mud from my wheels while other drivers went past and laughed in their 4x4s. Sometimes they would offer me a lift, but I was enjoying the challenge as the mud would go all the way up to my knees as I pushed the bike through the swamp.

A change in landscape makes a huge difference to the rider on a bike tour. While it was difficult to avoid boredom at times on the long, straight roads like the ones I rode in Chile, Peru offered a multitude of climates and landscapes which kept things interesting. I moved from the mountains to the jungle because I wanted a new experience, to eat different foods and see something new. I found it really enjoyable and it rejuvenated my spirit, but after two weeks, I realised the mud made the flat roads slow going and tedious, and I was ready to return to the mountains. Climbing high has never been a problem for me and I crossed the Andes about ten times in total in South America. I enjoyed the climbing, and as an optimist believed what goes up must come down! I was now headed back up to the mountains and was going to cycle over the highest pass of the whole trip. I was aiming for a town called Huaraz in a region called the Cordillera Blanca.

The Cordillera Blanca is famous for tall majestic white peaks which look out over Peru and contain the highest peak in Peru, Huascaran, at 6700 metres. The mountains look inviting and dangerous in equal measure. There are four roads which cross the divide, and most are sealed, but the most challenging route over the range, called the Huayhush road, runs between Hullanca and Huaraz and is just a rough track I looked at the different routes and thought to myself *why take the easy option when I can try the hardest?*

The tarmac wound up to 4000 metres before I reached the turn-off, which was a two-metre wide rocky track with loose compacted stones. The sign told me to watch out for landslides and just ahead of me I could tell why: fallen rocks and rubble had cascaded over the track, blocking it off, meaning cars and vehicles would not be able to pass. I was able to carefully pick my way around the landslide, pleased that I would have car-free travel over the rest of the range. It was slow and steady cycling since it was off-road, but it was stunning, with the silence and isolation giving me the feeling of being a bicycle mountaineer.

I cycled over the top of the pass which sat at 4950 metres, the highest elevation of the whole trip. I cooked some pasta at 4800 metres which was the highest I had ever had my lunch, and it was great to see my trusty MSR Whisperlite stove working at such an altitude. The rocks continued on the way down the pass and became pretty loose as I descended past a large glacier. The bike would often slip sideways, and I had to either grip my brakes hard or walk the bike down to avoid falling. It was fun, and I found myself grinning as I slip-slided my way down, the black rocks pointing skywards beside me.

Once I got down to around 3500 metres, the conditions became a lot better, and I cycled through a beautiful national park full of Puya Raimondii trees. These strange-looking trees look like they are planted upside down with a large bush of spikey vegetation at the bottom and a long stalk sticking up out of it, over three metres high. It was not long before I finished my off-road pass and I was back on the tarmac, on the other side of the national park. I camped that night with the high peaks of the mountains behind me, and it was glorious to ride among them in the next few days. I loved being able to see nature up close like that.

Being alone in nature is really good for the soul, and I got such a thrill from being up in the high mountains. Living on my wits and taking in all the impressive sights calmed me down and made me reflect on my journey. I had come such a long way, and now I was over the highest point of the whole trip. It really was all downhill from here.

Leaving the Cordillera Blanca behind, it was time to go and visit the next region of Peru and stay in the Casa de Ciclista in Trujillo on the coast. My bike needed some new parts, a new chain and casette and since the casa here had a little workspace where I could make the necessary repairs, I decided to head back out of the mountains onto the flat land again. The coastal region is also the most dangerous with lots of reports of cyclists getting robbed at gunpoint as they cycle along the sugar cane producing coastal area. I even met a young German who told me how he was held at gunpoint just north of Trujillo when a motortaxi forced him into the cane and took his bike and all his valuable possessions. There are lots of horror stories about people getting robbed, but nobody publishes a report to say how many people are *not* robbed travelling through that area, so I was cautiously optimistic that I would be alright.

I reached the coastal town of Chimbote with no problems, and slept within the sugar cane, out of sight of anybody. The following day I stopped to buy some bread from a roadside market stall in a small village and was having a laugh with the attractive young Peruvian girl selling the bread. As we were laughing, I could see some guys in the corner of my eye getting agitated with me, so I said my goodbyes, and as I cycled past the group of guys, they were all staring at me with their scarves pulled over their faces. I stared back, and they all jumped into their motortaxi at once. I thought, *Oh shit, I'm in trouble now*. I rode straight, and I rode fast. Not wanting to be stopped, I carried on without looking behind me, thoughts of whether I could defend myself with the little multi-tool I kept in my bar bag flashing through my head.

Luckily, they soon gave up the chase and turned around. I'll never know whether the danger was real or whether I had misread the situation, fuelled by the stories I'd heard and articles I'd read before I set off. As with most topics, what you read online is biased and can be sensationalist: no-one writes about an uneventful journey through a relatively uninteresting part of Peru. While it is sensible to be aware of the potential dangers and take necessary precautions before travelling somewhere like this, I still believe there are relatively few people who are truly malicious and a threat to your safety, and it shouldn't stop you visiting.

Once I arrived in Trujillo, I knocked on the door of the casa to see Greg and Morgane there. It was great to see them again, another random encounter of the cyclist world. The owner of the casa was away, but I was made to feel at home with good friends and stayed for about three days while I fixed the bike. All ready and new, it was time to cycle the last part of my route through Peru and head once more back into the Andes before making my way to the border of Ecuador. I wanted to take the mountain border as the heavy traffic along the coastal road made for unfriendly and unexciting riding. As soon as I was in the mountains, the traffic noise suddenly subsided, and I could think clearly again.

My last few days in Peru went by with only one moment of excitement as I was camping just off the road on a small escarpment behind a rock, next to but hidden from the traffic. It was maybe 5 p.m., and the sun was still shining as I stopped, set up camp and rested before starting to cook. The golden light of sunset was about to descend upon me, and two older Peruvian men staggered up the side of the bluff. They must have been surprised to see me, but they came over, and I soon saw that both were very drunk. They had a bottle of home-made alcohol with them and offered me some. Not wanting to appear rude, I drank with them. While I was happily chatting to the younger man, his older friend stood behind him and made cut throat motions with his hand across his neck, before aggressively pointing at me. He was in his late fifties and very drunk, so I was not scared, but it was an intimidating gesture. His friend was the opposite, friendly and chatty. I had to make a call. Since they were both so drunk, it was hard work to keep up the conversation, and after seeing this level of aggression I did not want to drink with them any more. I asked them to leave and they both staggered back down the hill, but the older man's aggression stayed with me all night. I considered whether I should move my camp spot, but a combination of tiredness and stubbornness meant I stayed put and luckily they did not return. I did not, however, sleep well that night.

Reaching the border with Ecuador, I spent the very last of my Peruvian money in the border town, buying some bread and biscuits. The next town was about 25 kilometres into Ecuador, but the roads were unpaved and steep, so I expected this to take a few hours. No problem, I was sure this town would have a cashpoint so I could stock up on cash and food again. The border road took me five hours to go 25 kilometres. The smooth 5% inclines of Peru were instantly replaced by 15% hairpins on which I had no option but to push. The road leaving the border was unpaved and made of clay, meaning it was slippery and had no grip. As the rain started to fall, I was battling hard just to walk upright, let alone cycle. It was a real test of character and resilience. Frustration and concern replaced my excitement and wonder of crossing the border and seeing a new landscape. I ate all my food reserves in the first hour, and reached the town of Zumba later that day, hungry and exhausted.

I stopped into a hostel and tried to book a room, but they would only accept cash, so I left the bike and went to go and use the only cashpoint in the town. Upon arrival at the machine, I quickly found that this was a local-only cashpoint and did not support Visa or MasterCard, so I was unable to use it. Dejected, I returned to the hostel and tried to call my bank to see if they could authorise payment but it was impossible. However, they said they had a cashpoint in Vilcabamba, a tourist town another 125 kilometres north. I did not want to go back to the border, so I went to try to buy a bus ticket to Vilcabamba, but again they only accepted cash. How I wished for my American dollars, but I had nothing. I didn't know what to do. If I continued on that steep, wet road, it would take me two days to reach the town, I had no money for food, and I was already hungry. Leaving my bike outside, I tried to explain my position to the lady in the bus terminal, but my Spanish did not extend to telling her the full story. I tried to get across that I would pay in Vilcabamba, and I think she understood, or at least understood that I needed her help, so thankfully she gave me a ticket. I think she saw the desperation or hunger in my face. I thanked her, then sheepishly showed her the bike and she laughed. I had a few hours to wait for the bus, but I was going to be alright.

It shows the reliance we have on money, and even in a modern country like Ecuador, you cannot take things like cashpoints for granted. I had become complacent and should really have had some US dollars as a backup. If it wasn't for the kindness of the Trans-Ecuador bus company, I would have had to go back to Peru and use a cashpoint there. I would not have died, but would have been hungry and upset. Luckily, people were out there to help. On arrival in Vilcabamba, I went to use the cashpoint to pay the bus driver, but since they were running late, he just drove off in a cloud of smoke behind me, so I never did buy that ticket. I took out some money and found a burger stand still open even though it was 2 a.m. and bought a big burger with all the extras before checking into a 24-hour hostel. Sometimes, even I will admit that it is ideal to be in tourist places, since everything is open all the time to get some of that tourist money! I fell into my bed and crashed out, happy to have made it, and ready for a belated border crossing beer the following day.

Vilcabamba is a pretty little village situated at around 1500 metres, ensuring it gets warm weather all year round. Due to its climate and affordability, it seems to be a central refuge for American expats in Ecuador with lots of middle-aged retirees living here. This made it seem quite out of place as there were more white people here than locals, and everyone was speaking English. It is pleasant enough if you like that sort of thing, but I was looking for something more authentic so, after a day's rest I headed north. Ecuador, like Peru, has three main arterial roads. You have a choice of beach, mountain, or jungle. As the mountain roads in Ecuador are incredibly steep and the beach roads too busy, I opted for the jungle road for the majority of my cycling in Ecuador. I liked the jungle roads, and felt drawn to the unexplored wilderness where the real adventurers go! I have read a lot of books about people slashing a path through the jungle with their machetes, and so this environment held a great appeal to me. Even though my adventure was much easier than theirs, with a lot less danger, as I slept each night in the jungle I would feel an affinity with those explorers who were inching their way forward to a new land.

I followed the Pastaza River, which flows from the mountains in Banos all the way to the Amazon basin. Each night I would be able to pull off the road and find somewhere to camp. It was great camping, with river access and palm trees. I sometimes even spotted an occasional papaya tree if I was lucky and would feast on the delicious fresh fruit.

I was about a three day ride from Puyo when I pulled off the road at around 4 p.m. one evening to set up camp by the river. I found a secluded spot between some trees and put my tent up before sitting in the shade and making some dinner. I saw some large ants on the ground, but my tent had a mesh inner, so I knew they could not get in. I ate my dinner away from my tent and sat out listening to the river before going to bed. It was so peaceful there by the river, and even as I sat in my tent that evening, I slowly fell asleep to the sound of the river going by.

I awoke late into the night. It was dark, and I opened one eye to see a large ant next to my head. *How did you get in*? I thought, and as I sat up to let him out, I saw two more in the tent with me. I turned on my light to see that the ants had chewed a hole in the side of my tent. And as I looked around, I noticed that there was now about six holes, each about an inch or two wide on both sides of the tent. I was under attack from leaf cutter ants, and they were taking the sides of my $300 tent to build their nest with! I jumped out and saw a line of ants all coming for the tent and knew I had to move, so I emptied the tent out and hauled it away some 300 metres from the line of attack. Leafcutter ants are fascinating as they all move in unison with small parts of leaves on their backs taking them back to their nests, but they are dramatically less impressive when the leaf is replaced with bits of my tent. To distract them from attacking me in my new location, I left a cotton sheet on a rock next to where my tent was so they could build their nest from this. In the morning, I surveyed the damage. I had two large holes and four small holes across both sides of the walls of the tent. I went back to look at the cotton sheet, and they had taken about an inch off the bottom of that too. There was nothing else to do but laugh: I had been camping in the jungle for months, and this was the first time I had come under attack from any animal. It turns out that it is not the people or the large animals which you need to worry about, but ants. I cycled off that morning to the next town where I bought a roll of duct tape and patched up all the holes. The tent would no longer be waterproof, but it should keep the insects out and only had to last me another five months.

*Chapter Seventeen*
# TIME

The end was in sight at this stage of the trip. I was thinking a lot about what it would be like to stop cycling. On the one hand, I was ready to stop: I had been cycling around the world for two and a half years now, and I missed family and friends and wanted to feel a sense of community again. A community is the one thing you miss when cycling long distances as you are never able to put down proper roots. You cannot engage in projects or work long-term if you have to leave every few days. Your sense of purpose is to cycle, and the ambition to keep moving forward gives your life an impetus, but real connections are things which take time, and that just isn't possible when you are on the road. On the other hand, if I stopped, would I get bored with life? For the last 900 days, I had spent nearly every one moving forward, seeing new things and experiencing new places. It scared me a little to think about just stopping. Would I be able to? I had read a lot about post-trip depression, and this is something I wanted to avoid. I knew that my life had taken a new path, and I had to follow this path and see where it would take me even when I returned home to England. This would be altogether another adventure.

This was on my mind going north along the river, and in an effort to establish a sense of community I had arranged a short volunteer project at a monkey sanctuary just east of the jungle town of Puyo. This, I hoped, would give me a chance to take a break and connect with a project, helping rescue orphaned monkeys and snakes from the local area. I knew I could only give a few days, but it was a great insight into the work they do and how they are helping their local environment.

I arrived and was greeted by the current volunteers who showed me around the complex. It had been designed by a tall Swiss man named Ivan, who had sweeping long hair and loved animals. At the complex, the monkeys had sprawling cages which ran across kilometres, all interlinked with tunnels and play areas. It was bigger than some zoos I had visited and you could see that real care and love has been put into the place. There were about 10 species of monkey, some snakes, lizards and even two tigrillos: spotted cats which looked like small leopards which we fed with live chickens each night.

I asked to camp as I did not want to pay for accommodation and was shown to the camping area. I looked down and running along in a straight line across the small pitch area was a line of leafcutter ants. I was not about to be under attack again so I quickly asked to camp indoors on my mattress instead. Everyone laughed at the idea of the ants being what I was scared of most. Ants and spiders. The sanctuary was deep into the jungle of Puyo, and everything was hand-built and did not quite fit, including the doors which did not go all the way down to the floor, leaving about a 6-inch gap. One night before I went to bed, a tarantula scuttled into the room where I was about to sleep. Shocked by the spider's boldness wandering into my bedroom and also scared to get too close to it, I backed out quickly before asking Ivan to move it. "I can move this one, but who will move the others that will come in during the night?" he asked me in his French-Spanish accent. So I spent the night waking up every few hours convinced a spider was crawling across my face.

I stayed here for four days, and my duties mainly involved feeding the monkeys twice a day. They ate fruit, mostly melon, banana and papaya. Ivan told me he purchased a whole stem of 200 mini bananas for just five dollars, meaning we could eat as many as we wanted, so the volunteers had fruit salad for lunch every day. On day three, we shared the fruit with a roaming battalion of army ants. Army ants move in groups of thousands and are very aggressive meat eaters. For two days, they came through the fruit storage, eating all the cockroaches. I still shudder to remember the painful bites as they ran up my leg into my boots and attacked me too. It was like a swarm, and I had never seen such aggressive actions by insects. Ants really were much more hazardous than the tarantulas which just seemed to come in and sit on the wall.

At the monkey sanctuary I had worked and assisted both Ivan and the animals. It felt good to be part of something, and being involved in the daily feeding routine allowed me to connect with the other people at the sanctuary. It gave me a small sense of the community in which I was looking for and gave me inspiration for what my life might be like after I reached Reading. I said my goodbyes to Ivan and the staff, checked my sleeping bag for any stray insects and headed back onto the road.

It was two days before the border with Colombia when I pulled off the road at around 3 p.m. to rest. I found a great little camping spot just off the road in an area which must have been an old quarry. I walked across the quarry and pitched my tent before climbing inside to read as there were too many sand flies nipping at my ankles to sit outside. After a few moments, I saw some movement out of the corner of my eye, and another cyclist had also pulled into the same quarry. I pulled on some long trousers before going out to say hello. His name was Robert from Poland, and he was also going north, so after a shared dinner, we agreed to cycle to Colombia together. I was always so impressed with the compatibility of the cyclists I met in South America. Everyone seemed to be on a similar budget and wanting to ride at roughly the same speed and distance.

We were both excited to see Colombia, a country which has had a lot of its recent political and drug history documented in the popular show *Narcos*. First, we stayed with a WarmShowers host just past the border in a town of Ipales and spent the night in his garage which had its fair share of rats. We had to stay in the tents inside to ensure the rats did not nibble on our fingers or toes during the night. I was becoming more feral and comfortable with being able to sleep anywhere, even with the possibility of rats biting me. The evening was a great introduction to the hospitality and friendliness of the Colombian people as we shared a family meal before going out for the traditional Colombian breakfast of rice, beans, chips and meat the next day.

Our destination was the town of Pasto before cycling over the famous Trampoline del Muerte or "Road of Death" in English. Unlike the more famous road of death in Bolivia, this road is even more dangerous since it is not closed to traffic and you often turn a corner, to see a bus or truck rushing towards you on narrow mountain roads. The road is also completely unpaved and only about three metres wide, so I have no idea how trucks pass each other without falling the 1500 metres off the edge to their death. Broken barriers and warning signs are a testament that you should proceed with caution. On a bicycle, however, you are relatively safe and I soon got used to the narrow width of the rocky terrain with the treacherous drop to my right side.

It was slow going, but the road of death was really the road of mild annoyance, since the bumpy ground would make my teeth rattle and my arms ache on the sharp descents. It was beautiful as the road rose up to around 2500 metres with the thin jungle clouds making contrasting shapes over the edge of the drop. There was also plenty of running water from waterfalls and streams, along with wild horses and nice little pull-offs which made great wild camping sites. The weather was also much more pleasant at this altitude. It was quite a shock to come back down to sea level with temperatures of 35 degrees.

We reached Macao on the other side, and it was the humidity that was killing us. It was OK if we were cycling as it created a cool breeze, but once we stopped we instantly became soaked in our own sweat. When camping, it got pretty disgusting in my tent and I would have to put a towel down between my back and mattress as the sweat poured off me.

For relief from the heat, we would often stop for a cold drink or some fresh fruit. Coffee was about 25p per cup. Sugar was always added, which was not to my taste, but it was very cheap and authentic coming from the coffee plantations on the other side of the country. Food was also very affordable with bakeries in every small village selling all manner of bread and pastries. It was good that Colombia was cheap as my money was running out and after looking at my bank balance, I had about £800 to cover the remaining five months, and I still hadn't booked my flight home. This was just about enough, but I would have to ensure I had enough to cover the expensive boat ride between Colombia and Panama and enough to spend in the USA, where things would inevitably be more expensive. This meant a continuation of my wild camping and eating cheap food, something that I think was also rubbing off on Robert. He had more money than me as he was planning on going further, but was still on a tight budget and I was able to teach him the tricks of a cheap life on the road.

It was in Bogota that I received a message from my friend Sandeep that he was getting married at the end of April and asking if I would be able to make it. This message rang a bell deep within my soul and helped me gather my plans: I knew I had to be there. I had five months to cover 8000 kilometres, more than possible at my current pace, especially as there were no real mountain areas to cross. I had given myself nothing to aim for the last two and a half years, and was free to do what I wanted and go where I pleased, but now I had a deadline. It would be nearly three years to the day that I began my cycling journey and watching my two friends get married would be the perfect end to my trip. I replied that I would be able to go, and booked my flight home from New York. And so the date was set.

It was quite emotional to confirm the end date of my adventure, and I unexpectedly found myself excited to be able to go home and celebrate with them. I did not then know at that point that having a fixed end shackles the adventure in some ways, and meant that I had to turn down some roads and opportunities so I could arrive in New York in time. At first, the schedule felt rushed, and I felt a nervous energy which meant I had to be constantly moving forward. It started after having a lovely time in Bogota for two days. I would have liked to stay longer, but I felt I had to move on.

After cycling with Robert for two weeks, I wanted to be on my own again. When we reached Medellin, we both agreed to stay in different places, with me opting for the Casa de Ciclista and Robert staying with a friend. We hugged when our road split, but it felt right for me to be riding solo once more. There is something about the freedom of cycling alone which really resonated with me, and I think two weeks is a good amount of time to cycle with others before the idea of being alone started to appeal to me again. The grass is really always greener.

In Medellin, I stayed in the Casa de Ciclista for three days, and there was another cyclist also from Reading. It was a small world, after all. We enjoyed the temperate climate, partied, and explored the city, which it was clear had lasting effects in the wake of the terror caused by Pablo Escobar. After three days, I left for the coast to get to the port of Turbo. The wind was on my side and I was covering 130 kilometres each day. I was having a lovely time listening to music, singing as I rode, and sleeping in petrol stations. Going fast and far with the wind behind you really does make you feel like you are flying. With a big smile across my face, I reached the port of Turbo, from where I could catch a boat to Panama.

Turbo itself is a rough little town on the end of the Caribbean Sea, marking the end of the road. Due to the presence of the Darien rainforest, there is no direct road linking Panama and Columbia. The rainforest is too dangerous to cross since it is filled with drug runners and freedom fighters and would be incredibly hard work to pass through with a bike, so you are forced to either fly or get a series of boats from Columbia or Panama. The boat was cheaper and felt more like an adventure, so I took this option. I needed to get a series of three speedboats, then cycle though part of the Panamanian jungle before reaching Panama City. The first boat was a catamaran which took me from Turbo to Capurgana. Capurgana is a tourist beach town on the edge of Columbia and is a weed smoker's paradise with lots of hippies around and many opportunities to chill out with the backpacker community. I only stayed one day since this was not really my scene.

Whereas the first boat was a comfortable catamaran that took two hours and had sufficient space for me and the bike, the second boat was essentially a fishing boat with a massive engine on the back. The owner charged me $15 and strapped down the bike as the boat bounced off the waves in a stomach-churning 40 minute ride from Capurgana to Puerto Obaldia. There were five of us in the speedboat, all looking to reach Panama. At Puerto Obaldia, the two American backpackers were searched first, and they found weed in their bags, meaning we all had to be thoroughly searched. This was really annoying for me as I had six bags which needed going through.

The port town is essentially set up just to process goods and passports, and we still had to take another speedboat to Carti. This boat takes five hours and costs $110 plus $20 for the San Blas Island fee. This was the most expensive boat of the transit, and that is because there is only one boat which makes the trip. This boat has no set departure time, but we were lucky as when we arrived at the dock, we found it was due to leave in just a few hours. We were met at the dock by a man who guided us through the process. I am sure he took a cut of the large boat fee, but since this was the only way to get to Central America, they could charge whatever they wanted for the journey.

We loaded everything onto the boat, which was staffed by three Panamanian men, and I helped them lash the bike down to the boat. They told me it was going to be rough seas and they had better tie everything down well. We all loaded into the boat with our San Blas paperwork and sat on hard wooden benches with a plastic canopy above our heads to protect us from the sun. The boat ride was to take us through the communities of the San Blas Islands, a remote village away from the mainland on small Caribbean islands.

The boat started up, and it was plain sailing for the first 10 minutes as we quickly left the harbour. As soon as we hit the open ocean, the waves rocked off the hull of the boat, making us fly out of our seats and back down onto the wooden bench. It was a coastal roller coaster of punishment as our heads hit the canopy before our bums smacked back down onto the wooden bench. I was glad my bike was strapped down and wished I was too. I managed to get used to the bumps, but occasionally we went over a big one and were slung high into the air again. After about three hours of this expensive and uncomfortable boat ride, everything suddenly went calm, and the boat stopped out in the ocean. It was as we were alongside the beautiful San Blas Islands. "I just need to head inland to get fuel," the captain said. *No problem*, I thought, as we got to see the San Blas for free, which is usually a $200 tour from Columbia. We offloaded onto the island, and it was about an hour until the boat returned. It was quite exciting to be left alone in a house on a desert island. When the boat returned, the captain told us it was not the fuel but there was a problem with the engine, and they would have to fix it overnight. Alarm bells went off as I had read about boat captains leaving tourists stuck on desert islands and making them pay their way off them, but we had to trust the guys as there was nothing we could do. They agreed to take us to another deserted island where we would be able to camp overnight.

We arrived, and it was like a paradise island with palm trees and white golden sand, the water lapping at our toes and as I looked right, one of the older French passengers was having a swim naked! The boat captain went to the mainland and bought us food, and we had a little party on the island before the rain came.

These islands sell for millions of dollars and the current owners were renovating it, putting up structures to be able to house tourists. In a way, this was their opening night. Everything seemed well until the following morning. We waited patiently for the boat, but nobody came. Hours later and there was still no sign of the boat. We were officially stuck on an island with no sign of recovery. Luckily, I had some trusty porridge, so we ate that for breakfast and threw a Frisbee around. Island life would have been better had my bike not been on the boat. I was starting to get separation anxiety and would stare out over the open water to watch for any boats. It was my own fault as the captain had asked if I wanted to take the bike out, but after all the bumping around, I was too tired.

We were stranded. It was surprising how quickly the conversation turned to food and survival. It was about 1 p.m. when there was still no sign of a boat that we all started to get concerned. Had we been conned and left on a desert island? Personally, I thought it unlikely as it would be unusual to buy your captives dinner first, but perhaps this was the culture in Panama. Lucky for us we did not have to resort to cannibalism or any of the other survival strategies we had discussed, as the boat came in at around 3 p.m. with lots of apologies. I was relieved to see my bike still tied to the hull. The captain told us everything had been fixed and we were off once again bouncing towards Carti and the mainland. Two more hours of crashing against the waves, and we had arrived. After showing our passports and San Blas fee paperwork and having a meal in the ramshackle restaurant on the water, I was off to cycle into the jungle and start exploring Panama.

I had made it from the bottom to the top of South America. A continent with a dangerous reputation had only shown me love and affection. At times, I felt the loneliest I had ever been on the trip, but it also was a continent where I made friends for life. Of everywhere I travelled, this was my favourite continent. The variety of landscape, the ease of language (once you learn Spanish), delicious food and kind, friendly people. Cycling alone for the longest stretch of the trip also allowed me to think and grow in myself. Being self-reliant taught me so much about myself. South America was beautiful, but it was time to test myself again through what people described as the most dangerous part of the whole trip: Central America. With its drugs, guns and changing governments I was excited to see it all for myself. Bring it on!

## Chapter Eighteen
# CENTRAL AMERICA

The road to Panama City showed its two sides once I arrived off the boat. The road through the jungle was exciting though the rough off-road steep tracks made it hard work. I had to push the bike up the short steep climbs since the recent rain had left areas of soft mud, making it impossible to ride and twice as hard to walk. My flat-soled shoes slipped backwards as I tried to keep my grip and propel my heavy bike up the steep, wet ground. It took me two days to cover 28 kilometres to the main road. Halfway through the jungle, I had to show my dog-eared and ripped San Blas Island pass to the authorities in a little guard hut, which they looked at disapprovingly before passing it around, laughing and finally letting me through. The bumpy boat ride had caused my pannier bags to open slightly letting in water and soaking my clothes, passport and Island pass, all of which were now more than a little worse for wear.

I camped that night in the jungle on the top of a remote ridge. It was a beautiful first wild campsite in Panama, so distant and exciting and worlds away from civilisation. I could hear the howling of the monkeys, and breathe in the fresh, moist jungle air. It was my favourite place to camp in Panama because as soon as I was out of this small border road and onto the main highway, I was immediately hit with traffic, noise, pollution and activity. It was such a sudden contrast to the peaceful jungle beforehand.

As I got closer to Panama, the road became more dangerous with lots of close passing traffic and times where there was no shoulder. I had to ride in the right-hand lane alongside fast-moving traffic, and I repeatedly shouted at passing cars and trucks, which gave me no room. I felt so small and vulnerable as the cars whizzed past like they did not notice me. Panama City is a large metropolitan city and felt much more Americanised than the big cities in South America. You cycle past large malls, and fast food chains and the skyscrapers block all the sunlight from reaching the depths of the city at ground level. I did not enjoy it and only stayed for one night in a small hostel where I had my border crossing beer. With the upcoming date of my departure back to England, I decided I did not want to hang around in places that held no appeal for me, so I hopped back on the bike and risked my life again leaving the city on the busy highway. Panama is a short and flat country, and I kept to the Pan-American highway as I headed north. I cycled past the Panama Canal on my way out of the city and stopped to watch all the giant ships sail through. The scale of the massive ships which passed through the small lock cutting out thousands of kilometres from their journey amazed me, and I stood at the wire fence watching the tugboats pull the giant cargo ships along.

Panama only took me a week to cycle through. With good quality roads, lots of traffic and some heavy rainfall, it was somewhat unremarkable. I would often sleep in small roadside churches under cover of their front porches. The weather was very humid, grey and wet but each small town or village had a church which was usually locked but provided a small concrete porch with rain cover. I would ask the neighbours if I could spend the night there and I was never refused by the kind people living next door.

After a week, I had reached the small city of David, where I noticed a small hole had appeared in the rim of my front wheel. This was caused by my rim brakes slowly wearing away the metal of the rim, and after 38,000 kilometres my front wheel had finally broken. The small hole was concerning as I did not know if the rim could collapse while I was cycling. I stopped the night there to get it fixed as I guessed it would be cheaper than doing it in the more expensive country of Costa Rica, which was where I was headed next. I saw there was a hostel in town, so I decided to head there for the night and fix the wheel the following day, but as I approached the location of the hostel shown on my map, I could not find it. I stopped and asked some locals if they knew where it was and they invited me for drinks and lunch of some rotisserie chicken. It was great to drink a few beers and chat with them, and it was not long before we were all quite drunk, and I had agreed to go to their friends' bar. Instead of going to the hostel, we went to a members' swimming pool, and I spent the day there with them drinking and joking around. One of the guys was from Alabama and had moved to be with his family in Panama. He helped me translate as we spent the afternoon partying. They were lovely people, and I felt welcomed and warm with their offer of hospitality. Sometimes you have an instant connection with the people you meet, and this was one of those times. Drinking and eating at the private swimming bar felt natural and comfortable, and I will remember my time in David fondly thanks to these guys.

Unfortunately, the good bike shop was not open the following morning, and the only other place with bike spares was a small garden centre and only sold cheap Chinese made wheels, which I did not think would last. I did not want to buy anything too cheap since I still had 7000 kilometres to go, and my preference was to buy a new rim and get someone to re-lace a new wheel. I cycled nervously to the border with Costa Rica and hoped it would not fall apart as I rode along on the busy roads. Luckily the wheel held and I arrived at my first Central American border crossing, which was a stark contrast to South American borders I'd crossed previously. Here, they charge you extra for all sorts of things like taxes, fees and stamps. It is essentially a tourist tax, and some borders cost more than others. The cost to enter Costa Rica was $10.

Once the formalities were over, I crossed into Costa Rica and found a small bike shop in the centre of the border town, Canoas. I showed the problem to the owner of the shop, but he just sold spares and could not do repairs. He did, however, have a large stock of wheel rims, and I managed to buy a new rim which would fit my hub and spokes, and he pointed me in the rough direction of a bike shop where I could get it remade. I cycled around to the bike shop which was really just a house with a small sign outside stating it was a 'Taller de Bicyclette'. I could see some bike tools behind locked gates, so I knew I was in the right place. I rang the door and woke up the mechanic who was fast asleep. It was 9 a.m., and he told me to come back in half an hour.

When I returned, there was a small queue outside of young boys wanting to get inner tubes replaced. I let them get their bikes fixed and then showed the man the problem. He looked at it and quoted me just five dollars, and it took him around 15 minutes to completely rebuild and true my new wheel. It was super service from a skilled professional who could have charged me a great deal more but didn't. Shops in Europe would not have been able to do this difficult task as quickly and accurately as this man working from his garage and it is a testament to the people of Central America that he charged me so little. I gave him $10 as I was so happy as I was able to continue and he could go back to bed.

Costa Rica was beautiful, and my first views were of large and expensive houses, palm tree fronted beaches and metre-long iguanas running up giant trees to escape the threat of the oncoming cyclist. It was postcard-pretty, and that meant things were also a lot more expensive here. It was the most expensive country I had visited since Argentina. The expense was mainly due to the cost of living being relatively high due to the amount of tourism. Costa Rica was booming with the most tourists of any Central American country. It has rainforests and beaches, and a lot of ties with Europe and the US, and their motto of Pura Vida (the good life) is clearly working to attract lots of visitors. I think the commercialisation is also due to their varied wildlife and subtropical weather systems matched by beautiful white beaches and cloud-covered jungle which makes for an attractive holiday package.

I stayed mostly in the lowlands but camped on the beach or close to it every night and had no problems, although I would occasionally meet some drunken locals asking for money. It seemed as if they were ignored and pushed aside by their country, as the government wanted to create a positive image that appeals more to the tourists. I did speak one morning with a very drunk man who expressed this sentiment and who was quite resentful of people coming to Costa Rica and not sharing their wealth with him. I offered him food, but he only wanted money and even drunkenly said he would fight me, before staggering off into the distance. I camped every night in Costa Rica due to the high cost of accommodation, meaning I was able to swim in the beautiful Pacific Ocean each night to clean off. It was the good life for me, but again it was pretty easy going and I pushed on, wanting to reach Nicaragua for Christmas.

For my third and final Christmas on the road, I wanted

to find a hostel and spend it with like-minded people. I had earmarked the town of Las Penitas for Christmas and booked a lively little beach hostel. Entering Nicaragua, I cycled through some beautiful scenery in the north with Volcanoes emerging from dense forest and lakes with clear, bright blue water and iguanas running for their lives up trees. I passed the twin volcanoes of Ometepe before cycling quickly in and out of the capital of Managua. Nicaragua is consistent with other Central American hospitality and beauty, with stunning views over Lago Xolotlan and some peaceful, free camping spots. As these countries are so small, you are able to see the quick and sudden differences between the nations, in particular as the commercialism of Costa Rica quickly gave way to the less touristy, lower-income Nicaraguan villages.

I quickly reached Leon and stopped for an ice cream before making my way down to Las Penitas for Christmas. I arrived on Christmas Eve at around 9 a.m. and surprised the sleepy hostel workers by asking for a beer on arrival. It was Christmas after all! There were maybe ten other travellers from around the world also staying there, and we all celebrated on both Christmas Eve and Christmas day with lots of beer and authentic Nicaraguan food of fried chicken tacos and rice. I was here for two days and left with quite the hangover on Boxing Day, but it was worth it for what was going to be my last Christmas on the road. I had spent the previous Christmases sick in China and being hosted by good friends Francis and Dean in Auckland for a family Christmas meal of delicious lamb accompanied by frozen cocktails, but I was looking forward to spending the next one with my friends and family in Reading. I had even already asked my mum to host it so I could recreate the Christmas of my childhood, although this time my nephews would be the ones being the centre of attention.

The next country on my route was Honduras, the 35th one I had visited. In the hostels, there was always a lot of talk about Honduras. As a country, it has had a complicated modern history, with many civil wars and military coups to overthrow governments. The latest conversation I'd had was about Honduras closing their borders to tourists due to a military uprising. I was more nervous about Honduras than any other country in Central America, and I was continuously reminded by people that this was the most dangerous part of the world. There are a lot of British television programmes showing the gang wars in Central America, mainly focused around Honduras and El Salvador, and this had worked to shape my expectations of these countries.

I arrived at Guasaule and found the border open and crossing it simple. Despite my fears, upon arrival in Honduras, I found a great country full of warmth, and it quickly shattered my preconceptions. I bought a huge watermelon for a dollar and was tucking into it when joined by a family in a small park. They had also bought melon for lunch, and we sat there in comfortable, companionable silence tucking into the juicy flesh of the fruit. Once we had finished, they told me that I was welcome in their country and to enjoy myself. I originally planned to get a hostel, but I felt comfortable, so I decided to wild camp in a small quarry just off the side of the road. I camped between some rocks and saw little lizards scatter as I moved around. I was not bothered or troubled during the night. In the morning I said hello to the neighbours on the side of the quarry, and they asked me if I camped there. I told them I had and they said it was not a problem and to enjoy my time here. I took the shortest crossing of Honduras and was across into El Salvador after just two days but felt like I would have liked to see more of this warm and friendly country.

I'd only been in El Salvador for two days before the accident that left me battered, bruised and without a bike. After being hit by the pickup truck, it took me a good while to get my confidence back on the bike. I was nervous and hesitated a lot. I would get angry quickly if a car drove by too fast and I had to stay in roadside accommodation to rest as I did not feel ready to camp. The mental effects of being hit lasted much longer than the physical ones, as even now I occasionally get flashbacks when accelerating fast downhill. All I could think about when going fast was the memory of the truck behind, and then me being in the hospital. It had scared me to my core, and I rode without my usual confidence. I would feel my body tense up, and quickly pull on the brakes to regain control and reduce speed. I was lucky that the coastal road in El Salvador was pretty flat, but it took me around two weeks to gain full cycling confidence again.

When I left the town of San Miguel, I only cycled 20 kilometres that first day. I needed to rest and recover but also wanted the freedoms of the road again. The following day I managed 30 kilometres, then another 30 kilometres the next, working my way up to 50 kilometres a day. I slowly increased my mileage in small increments, with each increase giving me a better feel for where my health and fitness levels were at. With each kilometre cycled, I started to gain my confidence back, began to get over the crash and put some distance both physically and mentally between myself and the scene.

I stayed in love motels along the road for the first three nights. Essentially these are sex hotels with large double beds and will occasionally have mirrors on the roof or poles in the room. I could usually negotiate a rate of around $10 per night, and they made perfect hotels for the single cyclist as they provided lots of privacy, with good Wi-Fi and hot water. It took me four days before I felt ready to camp. I found a spot just off the road which was in a large field between some trees. My confidence was low, but I knew I needed to build it back up, so I camped early and started to get back into the routine, tent first followed by dinner then relaxing before sleep. It was a bright night, and I awoke in the morning and felt better. I must have awoken about every two hours, but I was safe. It had been about three weeks since my last camp out, and it felt good to get back into the adventure lifestyle. It helped lift my spirit, and it kept me on the path to Reading, USA. When camping out in my tent, I always slept better than in a posh hotel. The fresh air and sounds of nature envelope me, and I sleep and rise with the sun which our ancestors must have done years ago. That morning as I rose at 6:30, I knew I had come through the worst of the crash and was now finally back on track. I had agreed to meet back up with Kenneth and Marie in Antigua, Guatemala in a few days, so I rode calmly and efficiently towards the border.

El Salvadoran roads are actually quite good in comparison to Guatemalan roads, and I could instantly feel the difference as I crossed the border and swerved and bounced along the potholed road. I was really looking forward to seeing my friends again since they had been with me at my worst. I looked forward to showing them my progress. I had agreed to meet up with them in a hostel called OX Base Camp, which offered the first night free if you arrived on a bike.

We continued to test my tenacity two days after my arrival with a demanding hike up the Acatenango Volcano. This famous two-day hike involved climbing the steep, almost vertical paths of Acatenango before settling into camp and watching the active volcano called Fuego erupt all through the night. Nature at its best, I thought, and since the volcano is free to hike without a guide, we departed on our own before hitch-hiking to the base of the volcano. The hike to the camp spot opposite Fuego was tough but beautiful. Especially at the beginning, it was very steep, and I think my legs were not really ready. I struggled, but with regular stops to take in the breath-taking views, we reached the top in perhaps four hours and set up our tents. We were right in front of Fuego, but luck was not on our side as the clouds moved in, and we could not see the volcano. We ate dinner and wished for the weather to clear, but to our dismay, it did not, and although we could hear the incredible power of Fuego cleaning out its lungs with loud booms, we did not get to witness the sight of the lava erupting. It was a bit of a shame, but we had tried and did not have the supplies to spend the night camping up there again hoping for the weather to clear, so instead we all got up at 4 a.m. to hike to the top of Atanegago to watch the sunrise.

The hike to the top was made much harder by taking a shortcut across soft sand, and I repeatedly slipped over. My legs hurt, and my pack was digging into my shoulders before Kenneth kindly offered to take my backpack. It was hard work, and we were making very slow progress until a group being led by a guide recommended we take their route. We agreed and met the group who all seemed surprised we had hiked here alone. In trainers. With phones for torches. I was great at cycling but not so hot at hiking it seemed especially hard after coming out of the hospital just four weeks prior. We followed the group along the easier well-beaten path and reached the summit of the volcano just before sunrise. Unfortunately, the cloud cover had not cleared, and the sunrise was hidden behind the grey mist all around us.

The temperatures were below freezing so we did not stay long, and as soon as it was light, we made our descent. The going down was just as painful on my legs as it was working muscles that had not been used in over two years. I would be in considerable pain following this hike for about three days, and I could not walk straight the following day. I hobbled about the hostel and as I went out for dinner with Kenneth and Marie. I was in the worst condition out of the three of us. It was a great little side trip, and even though my legs and I were totally unprepared, it was a great hike, and I look back upon those days with real joy. It was tough, but I really enjoyed the harder moments. There is a real sense of accomplishment having scaled the volcano, and even though we did not see the eruption, we made up for it with good company and shared memories. I also felt that I could achieve anything, and it helped a lot with my confidence in being able to push my body following the crash. It was hard, and when my feet were slipping in the sand, I struggled, but I pushed on and made it up. I now knew that I could make it across to Reading, I just knew in my soul this journey would be finished. Sometimes it is good to be on your own, but there are times when you need others around you to help you and to push you. If I was on my own I likely would not have scaled the volcano as I would have been too unsure of my abilities, but with friends, I was able to, and I am so glad they gave me the confidence to carry on.

After about three days of rest, we were all able to continue as a threesome. We rode north towards the border with Mexico and around the beautiful Lago Atitlan. The famous alpine lake in the centre of Guatemala is a real sight to behold with beautiful blue water reflecting the image of the tall mountains across it. Some of the toughest hills of the trip for me were found alongside Lago Atitlan. Often

Kenneth and Marie would fly ahead with their lighter off-road bikes, and I was left chugging up the steep hills, occasionally pushing, as even though I had a super low gear, it was just too tough to climb. We cycled all around the lake taking in the beautiful colourful cemeteries juxtaposed against the grey concrete building for the living. We ate street food and even paid an emotional visit to San Simon, the patron saint of cigarettes and alcohol. I visited the saint and queued to say my prayer. As a non-religious man, I never felt a kinship to any idols, but I did want to say thank you to San Simon, a saint after my own heart. I bought a beer and drank some in the queue before splashing some on the figure of San Simon and saying thank you for keeping me alive before leaving him the rest of the beer. Just as we left, three mariachi arrived to play songs, and it felt good to say thank you to whatever might be out there and looking after me.

The rest of Guatemala was hard but not as bad as the roads around the lake, so we made good progress, camping in beautiful spots every night. It was not long before we reached the border with Mexico. Unfortunately, Kenneth got sick on the first night across the border, so he slept while Marie and I shared a bottle of Mexican beer with a lime in it, the proper way. With Kenneth feeling sick, we stopped for a few days in a hotel. I spent time writing blogs, resting, watching movies and eating tacos. The food was delicious and cheap, where we could often buy homemade tacos at five for a dollar. Mexican food had more flavour than the food of Central America with lots more spices included, and I enjoyed everything I ordered. The Central American hospitality continued with us staying with families and in police stations but it was not long before we were due to separate, with Kenneth and Marie headed inland while I was cycling the eastern route along the Gulf of Mexico. That morning we met a young local Mexican man in a small town we were staying in, who wanted to host us for breakfast. We quickly agreed and followed him. As we walked down the street back to his house, everyone looked out of their houses and shouted "Hola!". He beamed as he led the three gringos through the town, as if he was proud to have us. We shared a beautiful breakfast feast with his family. His mum, sister and dog were all home, and this man had such a friendly spirit. We spoke Spanish with the family and ate our fill of tacos, beans, rice and salsa.

We left with our hearts and bellies full before I had to say goodbye to Kenneth and Marie. It would be the last time I cycled with them on this trip, but we had became lasting friends. You go through a lot on bike tours and the connections you make last for life. It was sad to see them go, but I needed to head along the flatter coastal route to enable me to make my flight back to England. It did mean not cycling along Baja California and crossing the USA from coast to coast, but I didn't have enough money to last that long in the US. I only had about £300 left, so I decided to enter the USA in Brownsville, Texas, which is the border crossing furthest to the east.

*Chapter Nineteen*
# THE FIRST WORLD

My last meal in Mexico was the perfect breakfast of rice, beans, tacos and coffee, and I was filled up and ready to cycle over the border into the USA. This was the largest, most secure and official border crossing I had seen, with miles of twin lined fence topped with razor wire separating the two countries. There is also a large bridge you must cross with armed guards walking up and down the pavement. The line between South America and North America had never been marked so clearly. In my confusion, I did not see anywhere to get my stamp out of Mexico, so I kept cycling forward, the only direction allowed and arrived at the official border of the US. I pushed my bike into the large building and walked up to the man at the front desk. He was dressed sharply in uniform, with neat black hair and a small moustache. He gave a disapproving look at me and my bike before I asked him where I could get an exit stamp from Mexico. "Sir, you are in the United States now," was his official response and seemingly he did not mind that I did not have the correct stamp from Mexico. Slightly surprised, I followed his direction into a smaller room with five other people, all of Hispanic origin and I had to tell my story to a lady at a small desk. She flicked through my passport, before asking me about my money, my work situation, how I would support myself. I was then told to re-purchase another ESTA visa even though I already had one, since I was not coming up on their system. I then had to wait another hour before a man approached and told me I could go. It was the longest and most dragged out border crossing since I had entered China. I did, however, not require an exit stamp from Mexico, and they never searched or checked my bags.

On the whole, it was a confusing and odd procedure. I entered the town of Brownsville, Texas, and the change from South America to North America was instant: chain restaurants, wide perfectly straight roads, the English language. It was exciting to be back in a country where people spoke English, but the formality and bureaucracy needed for me to cross the border was too much. My heart went out to those people from South and Central America who would likely be checked much more thoroughly than I had been.

I had lots of food on me from Mexico, so I didn't need to stop in Brownsville other than to collect some water and purchase a Krispy Kreme doughnut... this was America after all. I stopped in the small 7/11, and was surprised to find lots of sweets and candy and processed food all remarkably cheap. I purchased two doughnuts for around $1 and began tucking in. I laughed, as there was no more

American a purchase I could make after crossing into the first world. A freedom doughnut.

My route across the USA would see me follow the Southern Tier along the southern states. The Southern Tier is a famous route documented by the American Adventure Cycling Association. They publish a series of maps highlighting the best cycling routes to follow which avoid the main roads. I wanted to go along the south and visit the iconic southern states of Mississippi and Louisiana as they had much more cultural appeal for me than either Kansas or Iowa, and would hopefully mean finding lots of interesting people and culture. Leaving Brownsville is simple; the highway becomes smaller, and you can ride on a broad shoulder safely away from the trucks and cars.

I reached an area called Kingsville, a vast Texan ranch property covering 1500 square kilometres. Cycling alongside the fence line for 100 kilometres was pretty dull with only passing cars and the odd cow for company. There was little in the way of shops and even less in terms of good camping spots. I camped that night in the median, the area between a split in the road. It was wooded, and I could camp there easily. I had a good sleep, and that morning I awoke to misty fog all around me. I got up and packed away before attempting to make my breakfast, until realising I had very little in the way of petrol left. The stove would not pressurise and therefore I could not produce a flame. In my hunger, I decided to make a little controlled fire in the woods and dip a few sticks in petrol to help light it.

Due to the mist around me, the fire would quickly go out, so in a moment of desperation and stupidity, I decided to pour my last bit of petrol onto the dying flames. My brain screamed at me that this is not a good thing to do as I lifted the little petrol container over the small fire. Petrol flowed down onto the fire, and before I knew what had happened, the petrol canister was engulfed in flames. The flames rose up and covered my legs, setting fire to the nylon leg warmers I was wearing. Instinctively I dropped the canister and rolled onto my back, raising my legs out of the danger area. I looked down to see the nylon had caught, it was now rising up to my groin. I rolled over again and patted my legs with the panic of a bongo drummer playing for his life. The fire was out, but the plastic nylon material had burnt and stuck onto my left shin. The smell of burnt hair rose around the campsite, and I often wonder if any passing cars happened to witness the strange cyclist in the woods setting fire to himself.

It was a bad situation but could have been considerably worse. I had burns but only on my shin and the petrol canister and the fire had quickly burnt themselves out without causing any damage to the woodland. I was lucky that it was a cold and wet morning. A simple wrong decision can put you in real danger, and, ironically, I had been using this stove with no problems for nearly three years before regrettably deciding to pour petrol directly out of the canister. I could have and should have gone to find a hospital to get checked out, but I did not want to bother anyone with my stupidity. I packed up and patched up my leg with bandages from my medical kit, before jumping back on the bike to continue. I had some pain in my shin but nothing that would be too harmful, my pride taking more impact than anything else.

I had cycled for about an hour when I came to a border guard office with lots of policemen around. "Excuse me, Sir", the young border officer said. "We need to see your passport." I showed my passport to the man, and he looked me up and down before taking a long look at my bike. Before handing it back he asked me in a stern voice "were you sleeping in the woods last night, we drove past a campsite in the median this morning." I told him I was, before asking the guard if it was a crime. "No," he replied "But be careful, this is close to Mexico, and there are lots of bandits around here."

American policemen are the same as South American policemen in that they will always tell you there are bandits about, even when you're camping in the woods in the largest ranch in Texas. I didn't tell them about my fire incident, and they told me I could fill up my water bottles so I was happy with that. They took a photo and wished me luck.

I had finally reached a small town where I could purchase some food. I went into a petrol station, but before I did, I bashed my shin on my pedal. A typical cyclist injury but this time I popped a blister and some blood started to run down my shin. I wiped it up and went in to buy a Snickers and Coke, but I must have looked pretty rough, possibly the most homeless I had done at any point on the entire trip: with dirty clothes, a stink to match and blood running down my leg. The guy asked if I was alright and told me not to pay him anything for the snacks. It was a moment of real kindness, but I do wonder if this was in support for cycling or whether he took me for being homeless. Sometimes I wondered if there was a difference between the two. Perhaps the only difference was movement. I was homeless, but going somewhere new each day and therefore on a journey – whereas many of the homeless community in America can't afford to travel. We all ate the same cheap food and slept in tents under bridges. I was comfortable with this analogy, but the difference was that I was doing this out of choice where many others have no choice, and this is their last resort. I felt a kinship with the homeless community, especially in America as the contrast between the haves and have nots is so marked and noticeable. I thanked the garage attendant for his generosity and went back onto the bike to continue my homeless journey.

I reached the township of Kingsville and stayed with my first WarmShowers host in the US, a kind gentleman called Glen who lived alone in a large house in the suburbs. It was kind of Glen to host me, and he let me set up my tent on his front porch before we ate a home-cooked meal and drank some wine. It was nice to be able to share my story in English, as while my Spanish was at a passable level, I could never communicate the way I wanted to. Making jokes and using expressions in my mother tongue, the conversation was more natural than it ever could be in Spanish. Glen and

I spoke about America and Texas and cycling before he offered to let me do my washing. He showed me the washing machine and sitting on top of the machine was a handgun and a packet of ammunition. Shocked and surprised by its openness and location, I was taken aback. While guns are of course part of American culture, in England, they are not, and it was shocking to see one. Glen moved the gun away from the washing machine as he made a small joke about the vibrations setting it off. I laughed nervously, this was something I would just have to become accustomed to. It is the American way, and gun culture can be seen far and wide from the shooting range at the back of the shopping mall to the guy wearing a gun on his belt while he tucks into his McDonalds burger with his family. I was going to have to get used to them being around. Just don't leave them on the washing machine.

My Texan adventure continued to leave its mark on me as just one night after leaving Glen's house, I camped in a small woodland on the edge of a small town. It was a perfect campsite just off the road but with lots of small trees to keep me out of view. I set up camp and found a small orange tree, so I ate, rested and slept. The next morning, I emerged from the tent to take a pee. I was tired and bleary eyed from sleep and could not be bothered to put on my shoes. I went to the toilet, but as I returned, I felt an intense sharp stabbing pain right in the middle of my bare foot.. It hurt, and I lifted my right foot to reveal an angry-looking ant staring back up at me with its pincers out wide about to take another bite. I jumped back into my tent, zipped the mesh and looked at my now reddening and swelling foot. It really stung, and the pain radiated throughout my foot, getting worse as time wore on.

It was the worst animal bite I received on the whole trip, and again it was those annoying ants. A scourge of the trip. I sat in my tent for two hours nursing the pain with painkillers before I put on my shoes and packed up, being careful not to disturb any others. As I cycled away, it hurt every time I put pressure on my right foot to pedal, and I had to stop a few times throughout the day to rest it. The pain continued that day for twelve hours. I have no idea if it was a fire ant or a bullet ant, but it was small and black with two sharp pincers around its face. I could not believe my luck, I had avoided snakes and spiders in both Australia and the Peruvian jungle, but a tiny ant in Texas had bitten me. It reminded me again that I had to be vigilant in my camping routine, and that was the last time I would walk around barefoot outside the tent.

I camped a lot in America due to the high cost of hotels. Whereas in South America I could take a hostel every few days for around $5, in America the average cost was $60 which was far outside my budget. I had about £200 to last the remaining two months and had to be very careful with my money. The good thing about America is that most towns had some kind of WarmShowers host, which meant that I was able to find a host every few days. I was able to stay in Rockport with Hugo on his boat, in Victoria with Gregory and his wife in their mobile home and in Houston in an apartment with Nathan. Staying with people meant I could relax, wash, clean and eat good food. I remember all the names and places I visited and the food we ate together. It is a really special thing for these people to open their homes to me, and this is a tradition which continued across America and which I am thankful for. There were often large distances between hosts in Texas, and this was perfect for me as I liked camp for a few days between each stay to maximise my personal time and have an element of freedom.

American food is restaurant food, no-one seems to cook. Each region has a local speciality and a meal can be actually quite expensive, costing upwards of $10–20 before drinks. When on the road, my tight budget meant that I had to cook my own food, and this meant shopping in supermarkets and dollar stores. The dollar stores were very cheap but only had packaged and processed foods. They were good for the packs of trail mix or high-calorie biscuits but did not stock any fruit or veg. The larger supermarkets are where I could find fruit and vegetables, but this was quite limiting in terms of budget. I remember trying to buy a day's worth of fresh fruit for less than five dollars and struggling. It was a marked contrast to South America where fruit and veg were cheap and readily available, while packaged food was expensive. It seemed backward and un-necessary, and as a result, I ate more packaged food and biscuits, and soon found I was actually putting on weight for the first time since Thailand. I had become quite skinny cycling over mountains and volcanoes, but I was currently cycling 100 kilometres per day and still putting on weight.

This was not a good sign for the quality of the food I was eating. Bread and bananas still were my favourite staple for lunch along with oatmeal and coffee for breakfast, but my dinners were becoming more of a rice and tinned veg variety rather than the fresh stuff, and I could feel it taking effect on me. Or maybe it was the vast quantities of biscuits I was also consuming!

I left Texas for the border of Louisiana and was excited for Cajun food and spices along with the creole culture of the south. I was not to be disappointed, especially as I cycled past all the crayfish farms. The Southern Tier route runs away from the highway and passes farmland towards the north, aiming for the township of De Ridder. De Ridder itself is only a small town, but I found real Southern hospitality in Mandie who hosted me and three other riders over two days along with her three large rescue dogs,. Surprisingly, Mandie was not even a cyclist herself; she just liked helping people. It was great to bond with the other cyclists who were travelling west and to share tips of the road over a few beers and home-cooked meals. It was a welcome break, and I was able to collect maps for the rest of the way as Mandie had a system for cyclists to leave and replace items for others that come in the opposite direction.

My real destination though, was New Orleans, a city I'd heard lots about and was excited to visit, and which would be the only place in America I would pay for my accommodation as I wanted to party and wanted to do it with other travellers. I left De Ridder and headed east towards Baton Rouge, where I was treated to a beautiful crawfish étouffée, by Mark, a cyclist activist and host there. A crawfish étouffée is crawfish and rice covered in rich, creamy Southern-style tomato sauce and was great to eat washed down with a few real ales. Mark also showed me the Louisiana state university which had a live tiger in a cage as their school mascot and a stadium with a capacity of 100,000 for university team American football. Local sports were big business in this part of the world. Cycling down the Mississippi was beautiful with cycle paths up high along the famous river, and it was not long until I had arrived in New Orleans.

I cycled into my hostel at around midday. I always liked to arrive in cities where I had to pay for accommodation at around noon as that way you get the full time there for your money. Upon arrival, I showered and unpacked and was going to make the most of my two days in the party city, so I went exploring straight away. It was so fun to walk around, drink beer and see the sights, and once I got onto Bourbon Street, New Orleans came alive. There was jazz on the street corners, people performing poetry, voodoo shops, and you could walk around with your beer in a paper bag; it was a playground for adults who liked to party, and I went into full-on party mode. I walked up and down, drinking and watching live music before returning to the hostel to meet people and drink some more. In the evening the hostel party was in full swing, so I sat there and ordered a shrimp gumbo and drank and chatted with people from around the world. It was fun, and it was not long until we were back on Bourbon Street partying and dancing. The following day was spent doing exactly the same but with a hangover and I could see how intoxicating the spirit of New Orleans was. It was fun and exciting, and that night we went out with even more people from the hostel. I was drinking beers from morning till night and could easily have stayed a few more days – but I knew when I got into that frame of mind, it is better to leave sooner rather than later otherwise I could go down the rabbit hole for a week or more and spend all my money. This city has charm and excitement and music and would make the perfect place to spend a summer in. I cycled away with fond memories and a headache. I was starting to get into a routine in America, and it was good to break that routine in New Orleans, but I needed to carry on heading east to get to Reading by the end of April. I had about two months left to cover approximately 2500 kilometres, My average cycling had been 1500 kilometres per month, and with no mountains and a well-conditioned road network, I knew I would make it in time. This led me to take a prettier route along the southern states of Alabama and Tennessee.

While cycling along the ocean, I stopped late one night to see if I could camp in town. I knocked on the door of the fire station but being a small town it was not staffed at night, so I set up camp in the corner of a large field opposite. I had just had dinner and was actually sitting in my tent when a police car turned up and drove onto the field. "Sir, come out of the tent," two uniformed police officers asked me in a broad southern accent. I quickly got my things together and popped my head out. "Have you got any guns?" I was asked before replying "Me? No! I'm English!" The policeman laughed and realised I was no threat. They did not allow me to camp there but recommended somewhere out of the town which was not private property and I thanked them before packing up. They were good guys, and I was starting to be more aware of the property rules in towns of the USA, which were much more strict than those elsewhere. Every part of the land is owned by someone, which is fine if I could track down the landowner but this was sometimes impossible. Churches were also another good place to spend the night, as usually, nobody was there after dark so it was unlikely I would be caught and asked to move on.

I remember having lunch on a bench by a church in Alabama when the pastor came out and asked me what I was doing. After hearing my tales of cycling he went into his car and retrieved a box of doughnuts and a hardback copy of the Bible. "These two will see you right," he says, before leaving me with the most American of roadside gifts. Luckily I was able to pass the Bible onto a host sometime later, as it was heavy and I would not read it. I did, however, eat all the doughnuts.

By the time I had reached the border with Florida, I had settled into a routine which included a lot of riding along the coast. The wind was getting up and was making forward progress tough, but this was a small price to pay for the warmer weather which you can find along the Gulf of Mexico. I had just taken a free ferry across from the beautiful Dauphin Island to Fort Morgan and met another cyclist there by the name of Mark. Mark was a long-haired energetic man from Minnesota who was spending his summer in the warm weather. We cycled along chatting and exchanging stories before Mark asked if I needed anything. In my typical Britishness, I told him I was fine, but my rear tyre was very worn, and he noticed that I was missing a few spokes. Mark kindly took me to Walmart and bought me the final rear tyre I would need on the trip, before cycling with me to a bike shop and getting some new spokes fitted. Then that night I received an email from Mark asking me to join him for breakfast. We met at a restaurant on the state border, and he treated me to a traditional Southern breakfast of grits and eggs with cheese. It was my first time to try grits, which is similar in appearance to mashed potatoes but with the consistency of porridge made with corn rather than oats. A true road angel. It is people and hospitality like this that exist all over the south of the USA.

A bike trip is made by the people, and being a good guest is just as important as it is to be a good host. I struggled with saying yes to things and accepting gifts at the beginning of the trip but soon became accustomed to accepting offers of food or shelter as people really wanted to both help and learn about me and my travels. America is a much richer country than say Mexico or Argentina, and often people wanted to give me money, including Mark who gave me a $40 donation to the trip. It took me a while to get used to this, but I was thankful for each cash donation in America, as it was essential to me as I was running out of money approaching Florida.

I soon arrived in Tallahassee, located in central Florida along the Panhandle and spent two days staying with Scot Benson who runs a property called the bicycle house. The bicycle house is similar to the Casa de Ciclista model from South America, where you can just turn up. It is a charity which has volunteers who repair and work on bikes for both the public, and the homeless and refugee communities who need them. It was a great project, and Scot was a strong leader. It reminded me of the Reading Bicycle Kitchen where I used to volunteer and first built my touring bike, so it was great to spend two days here with this little community who had such a positive spirit. I was also able to work on my bike in a professional environment with the correct stands and tools. The bike itself was starting to fall apart, and at this stage, I was breaking spokes at a rate of around two per week. This was really serious, as it meant I would have to carry spare spokes around all the time and continually replace them. Sometimes the wobble due to the buckled rear wheel got so bad that I had to take off the back brakes entirely! In Tallahassee, I repaired all the spokes which were broken and got the wheel as straight as I could. I was sure it would then get me the remaining 2000 kilometres to Reading.

I continued east to Gainesville, where I had arranged to stay with Leif and Ashley, a couple I had met previously when staying in the Estrellita Hostel in Cusco, where we quickly became close before we went our separate ways. I had arrived on the same day they were due to go canoeing on the rivers of Florida. At first, I did not think I would make it in time to meet them, but as I rode into the large supermarket, I locked my bike and went inside before unexpectedly bumping into Leif in the bread aisle. We hugged and it was perfect timing as they were just purchasing supplies for a day on the water. We shopped before I loaded my bike and gear into the car and went straight out canoeing with them and their friends. It was a beautiful day with crystal clear water and bald eagles circling overhead. We had beers and told stories and went swimming. I went back with them to their house where I would spend the next three days.

Leif and Ashley taught me a lot during my time at their house. They took me dumpster diving for the first time ever, and we drove around Gainesville, hitting their favourite bins. All the dumpsters were outside major supermarkets and unlocked. We went at night to avoid detection. Part of me loved the idea that it was free food, sustainable and helped reduce waste from the supermarkets, but part of me also thought the idea of rooting through the bins to be pretty gross. That is until I tried it. We visited three bins that night and came away with a plethora of different goods. It was amazing to see what was being thrown out, and we must have returned with close to $100 worth of food. Bread, cakes, tinned goods, eggs, vegetables and cheese. All good to eat and the kitchen table looked like a presentation at the school harvest festival. While we were the obvious beneficiaries of this waste, it does highlight how much is wasted and simply thrown away when there is an ever-increasing number of homeless people. There must be a better way to deal with this waste rather than just to throw it away. Ashley and Leif did all of their shopping out of the dumpster, and it was clear to see why they were able to live cheaply and eat well at the same time. It was a great lesson, but I never had the confidence to do this on my own once I left them. I was happy enough with my routine, but it was certainly an eye-opener into another way of providing food.

In Gainesville, I was also introduced to another way of making money on a bike tour. Ashley and Leif owned a Pedicab business and on my last night in Gainesville I had the opportunity to work with them at a music event. I jumped at the chance, and spent my evening ferrying passengers back and forth from the car parks to the music event, making about $10 each time. It was a popular business, and I worked for about five hours and made around $180 in profit, after I paid Leif money for petrol and hire. I was over the moon as this made a massive difference to my remaining budget. In fact, it doubled it, meaning I could relax a bit on the money front. The work was enjoyable and the people kind and receptive, and I would often make a bit extra from tips. One guy even gave me $30 just to take him three miles away to his hotel on the other side of town. Unfortunately, the battery went flat part way there since this was my last drop, but after cycling for nearly three years, my legs were strong enough to take him to his hotel and back even without a motor!

I left Gainesville with my wallet and spirit full. Leif and Ashley rode me out of town and through the nature reserve where we saw a heron, snakes and alligators. It was a beautiful way to leave, and from that chance meeting in Peru, we had established a friendship which I remember fondly to this day. Gainesville is an energetic city full of northern Florida weirdness, mixed with southern hospitality and is the most liveable city I visited in the southern states. Just another 100 kilometres further and I had reached the Atlantic Ocean. I had rode into the township of St Augustine, which is famous for being the first place the Spanish landed back in 1565 and is the oldest European settlement found anywhere in the United States. For me, it was emotional as it meant I would change direction for the last time on the trip and point my bicycle north for the final push to Reading.

I still had 1600 kilometres to cover and just over a month left, so I was right on time. With the sea on my right, I made my way up the coast. I cycled past the beautiful town of Savannah which has an old-world feel, as it was a strategic town in the American Revolution. It has a large cobblestoned pedestrianised town centre where people sell artisan goods like homemade chocolate and ice cream. I stopped for a few free tastings but did not buy anything. It was busy and exciting with lots of people around, however, I did not stop and continued cycling over the large bridge over the river and onto the town of Charleston, where I had arranged to spend a few days with Melissa.

Melissa was a cycling activist and cycle tourer herself and worked with the Ted-X speaking community and the Charleston Moves campaign. I had a wonderful time staying with lovely Melissa, and we connected with a love for all things adventure and bicycle. We got very drunk at a tiki bar before spending the next day at an activism presentation trying to get the council to invest in more cycle safe routes in Charleston. It was a well-supported event and showed what can be achieved when people get together to support action; with the council promising to put money into the infrastructure. Charleston itself is a beautiful city winning many awards, and has moved on a long way from its history as an important port during the slave trade back in the 1800s. It is said that nearly half of all slaves brought from Africa arrived into Charleston before being moved on, and it is a testament to the city that it has many museums and memorials to its brutal history.

I set off from Charleston, and was really enjoying myself riding through Georgia and South Carolina, headed towards Georgetown where I had agreed to meet Mandie, my host from back in De Ridder. To get to Georgetown, I had to cycle past all the tall pines of Francis Marion national forest. It was fun cycling, with lots of routes into the woods where I could take a break in the long grass or set up a camp away from the road. I camped in the forest that night and was due to meet Mandie somewhere along the road the following day. It was 10 a.m., and I had been cycling for two hours and was ready for a break, so I pulled over and sat in the long grass in my loose cotton cycling shorts, enjoying a snack of bread and banana. After ten minutes I hopped back onto the bike and started cycling. About twenty minutes later, I could feel itching down below and stopped to investigate. I ducked back into the forest and had a feel around and felt some little lumps on my testicles. I went further into the woods to check properly and saw that about five ticks had buried their heads into my testicles. I felt sick, but there was nothing I could do but remove them as quickly as possible. I knew how to remove them after dealing with a dangerous paralysing tick in my upper thigh back in Australia in 2012. I learned that a pull and twist method was vital to remove the ticks alive, as you are at risk of infection if you pull out their bodies and the heads remain inside you. It was nasty work as I reached down and pulled the little critters out, but eventually I got all of them out. I think they must have been in the long grass when I stopped for lunch, and they moved in for their own lunch!

You need to be careful when in the long grass as ticks are prevalent and want nothing more than to crawl up to your groin or armpit and stick their head in. Once I pulled them all out, I had to have a laugh at my bad luck with bugs once again, before cycling on to meet Mandie. It was only about twenty minutes afterwards when I saw her car pull over in front of me, but I couldn't face telling her what had happened as it was a pretty gross thing to share. We rode into the town of Georgetown, where I washed my hands thoroughly before eating a traditional Southern meal of chicken and pigs foot rice with biscuits. That evening I camped outside of Georgetown but well away from the long grass!

The road north of Georgetown was impressive as I rode along smaller roads with the endless Atlantic Ocean to my right. The main highway went inland, so the secondary roads were lovely and quiet. There was a frustrating side wind, but the views made it worthwhile, as well as the range of free or low-cost ferries to get across the water when the road ends. I could tell I was continuing my journey north as it was starting to get colder and I had to ride in long trousers and a coat rather than the shorts and T-shirt of Florida. Soon I was riding on the outer banks of North Carolina along a thin coastal spit with waves crashing on the right and banks of white sand dunes on the left. The road was narrow but the traffic was light, as most of the homes are holiday homes or rentals for the busier summer period and were empty in late March. It was fun to hop on ferries and share tales of the road with the other passengers also on their own little adventures. I reached the town of Kill Devil Hills where the Wright brothers, the famous flight pioneers made their first successful flight. I stayed with Pat, another host so warm that she invited me into her lovely home as she was having a party with her friends. We shared stories and lots of delicious wine brought down from the Finger Lakes by her friends John and Susan.

Leaving the Outer Banks, I was getting close to Pennsylvania, and the realisation was that I was now in my last two weeks of this adventure. Part of me was ready for the trip to end, but my life on a bike was simple, and I loved it. There is a "no bad days mantra" which gets passed around, but cycling and camping and seeing new things every day really did hold that unique appeal for me. I was living, and I was nervous about what everyday life would be like. It was easy, however, to put thoughts of the future to the back of my mind when cycling as I could just look around, perhaps put on a podcast and move forward. Soon I had reached the capital of the United States, the stylish and cool city of Washington DC. I was staying in the north of the city for three days, and it was a mix of vibrancy and attitude which I loved. The Capitol Hill area seemed a world away from the edgy and exciting northern suburbs where I stayed. I spent two days exploring and it was really very pretty as the cherry trees blossomed and their pretty pink petals flew around in the brisk, windy air. Washington is surprisingly open, and I visited the Supreme Court and found a state senator in his office who did not mind giving me a pass to the Capitol Hill building to have a look around.

The sun came out in Washington, and after three days, I left to finish the final leg of my journey. It was approximately 200 kilometres to Reading, and I expected this to take three easy days due to the rolling Maryland hills. It was not long before I came to the sign for my final state border which was that of Pennsylvania and I was disappointed to find it was the smallest state border of the whole trip. Along the southern states, you have two-meter square road signs proclaiming a big welcome, along with a nice slogan or the name of the governor. But entering Pennsylvania, there was just a small, six-inch square sign attached to a post which simply said 'State Line'. Entering the final state was achieved with no triumphant exclamation, no sign to welcome me in but part of me liked it. It made sense to me that the trip was about to reach its conclusion with little fanfare. From the day of my leaving my home in Reading, to this day three years later, I had always played down the trip, and it looked like Pennsylvania shared my British sentiment of having a stiff upper lip. Who needs a party when you still have 150 kilometres to go anyway?

*Chapter Twenty:*

# THE FINISH LINE

After crossing the low-key state line, I passed into the final stretch, which would see me travel across Pennsylvania to Reading. I was prepared for what I expected to be an emotional but uneventful arrival. I only had to cover 100 kilometres, but I wanted to arrive into Reading at lunchtime, so I planned to take two and a half days, including stopping at my final WarmShowers host in York. I stayed with a lovely couple and spent the night there with another cyclist called Hiatt, who was just one week into his bike tour across America. It was a meeting of the minds and an excellent way to pass on my three-year experience to someone who had just started. He was a confident and committed young man, and I hope I helped him in some way.

I left my hosts in the morning heading towards Lancaster, a town only 60 kilometres from Reading. I decided to cancel a stay I had organised with another host, and instead chose to spend my final night before Reading on the road. It made sense that I spent it in the tent, as I had done for most of my trip. I wanted to spend time on my own, to cook and think, and reflect on the journey which had changed my life. I had become a different person. I could feel my spirit was lifted inside, and I was full of joy and positivity. When I was working, I could feel myself becoming low and depressed. I felt trapped with a reliance on money and accommodation. The only real experience I would get would be the weekly social nights down the local pub. Life felt stagnant, I didn't read, I watched too much TV, I dreamed but didn't believe I could make those dreams my reality. Now I was self-reliant; I had crossed deserts and mountains, I had survived being hit by a car, I had slept in storm drains and hadn't watched TV in years. I still dreamt; but now my dreams had become attainable as I had no fear any more. There is no need to be scared when you have lived. That night I found the perfect campsite, it was up on a ridge-way above the road, in some bushes well out of sight of anyone.

I set my tent up, and as I sat there, the temperature dropped, and it started to snow. I sat outside as the snowflakes fell around feeling very content. In my former life, I would never have contemplated sleeping outside in the snow for even a moment, but now it felt like second nature. As I sat there in the woods with the snowflakes raining down on me, I was happy. My final campsite was matched with a last dinner of pasta and pesto, and a cheeky beer to wash it all down. Living simply is something that had always appealed to me deep down. I had found on this trip that I was much happier and content with a simple life, rather than a complicated one. I didn't long for posh hotels,

I did not need lots of possessions and I did not understand the career-driven mindset of many. I am a simple person who was happiest when sitting in the snow with a pot of pasta and pesto, alone but content knowing that the next day I would cross the invisible finish line which had been my destination for three years. I was excited, and I was teary. I cried, thinking about my grandad. This was for him, and his memory stayed with me when I was always at my lowest. I thought of how strong Finola was to cycle halfway around the world and put up with me when our times were hardest. I reminisced about all the wonderful, kind people I had met and the hospitality shown to a random person on a heavy bike from a faraway country. When I set out, I had wanted to see if the world was a beautiful place, and now knew for myself that it was. Nature and humanity mixed together, to show me that if you go outside and explore, you can see how fully wonderful the world is.

That night my phone started to buzz. I looked over to see I was starting to get some messages from my Mum and Dad, who wished me congratulations, and wanted to know when and where I would be finishing tomorrow.

"Lunchtime," I replied before adding "Probably." My dad wanted more, "What time precisely?" "Ermm... Eleven or twelve, probably, I'm not sure" My plan was to just take a photo in the main square. "Can you please let us the exact time and place please?"

Something was up, and I was beginning to think that they might be in town. I did not want to get my hopes up for two reasons. If they were, I wanted any emotion to be real, and if they were not, then I didn't want to feel sad on a big and important day. I replied to my parents that I would finish at the Reading Pagoda at midday. The Reading Pagoda is a red four-metre high Japanese pagoda on the south side of town on a large hill, overlooking the rest of Reading below. It would make an excellent final destination point if my parents were in town, and it also had the words *City of Reading*, written below it making a good photo point regardless, especially since Reading has no central plaza, and the shops and restaurants are mainly located in off-site malls or along a busy main street.

With my destination and time set with Mum and Dad, I drank my beer on my hillside and had a peaceful night's sleep. Tomorrow this chapter of my life was about to end, and thoughts of this danced through my mind that night. I slept well and awoke ready to cycle the final 50 kilometres to Reading. It was a pretty uneventful ride, but I was smiling from ear to ear every inch of the way. I had imagined myself reaching Reading, and what that might feel like, and now what was previously imaginary was about to become real. In the days and weeks before I finished, people would always ask me why I was ending the adventure in Reading. The truth was that I just liked the way it sounded as a concept, from Reading to Reading, a full circle. I had never really envisioned what Reading, USA would actually be like. I was told that it was not a pretty, historic or iconic town, and innumerable people told me to finish in New York instead. Reading itself once had a proud history as a mining town, but once that industry closed down the city was left behind. The modernisation of surrounding megacities like Philadelphia and New York meant that they flourished, while Reading was left with poverty and community problems like homelessness and drugs. But in that understated way I enjoyed, it seemed a much more fitting end than New York.

I was about twenty miles from Reading when I heard the familiar hiss of air coming out of my front wheel. I had a flat, and upon further inspection, I had a hole in the side of my tyre. I actually managed to stop just outside a Dunkin Donuts, so I jumped off the bike and went inside for a coffee and doughnut before fixing the wheel. I patched the inner tube and put some old rubber between the tyre and the tube to cover the hole, but you could still see part of the inner tube poking out of the hole when inflated to the recommended pressure. This was dangerous and likely to lead to another flat, and I was forced to ride half inflated and slowly. But the final road was not meant to be too easy!

Soon I was seeing signs for Reading, and the miles were ticking down as I approached. I took a photo with every sign as I got nearer, and then all of a sudden, I had crossed a bridge and found the smallest sign which read "Welcome to Reading." I had arrived. I had made it. And with a single pedal stroke, I transitioned from being a cyclist who was cycling around the world to one who had just done so. I raised both hands in the air and celebrated, but I still had a final few kilometres to go before I reached the Reading

Pagoda. The road to the pagoda wound its way up a steep hill, and I cycled up and around slowly, savouring every last pedal stroke. I climbed until the road started to flatten out, letting me know I was at the top and as I snaked around the final bend, I saw a photographer, and I smiled. I knew this was going to be an emotional reunion.

I then saw the pagoda and tied to the sign was both a British and American flag, and underneath was my mum and dad beaming from ear to ear. I waved my hands in the air and cycled towards them, grinning back myself. It was great to see them there, and it felt like all the dreams I had over the past three years just exploded, as the local news crew took photos and videos of the final few hundred metres. I stopped and shouted, "I did it!" and hugged both my parents. Everybody was crying as I put the bike down to one side to properly embrace them both. I couldn't believe they had made the effort to fly out to meet me, and I realised it would have been quite an anti-climax to arrive into the centre of Reading alone. I had not seen my parents in nearly two years, so it was amazing that they were there to celebrate with me. I had often dreamed of the moment when I would finish, and I could not have planned it better. In my head, I would arrive into Reading, and after a quick photo, I would order some food and have a little cry over a beer before the inevitable cycle to the airport in New York. To share the moment meant so much, and as a mostly solo cyclist, I think it was even more special. I had thought a lot about being alone, and while I loved the adventure and freedom of cycling solo, my best and fondest memories were of times shared with others, whether it was with people I hardly knew or a long-time partner.

*Reading Eagle*, the local city newspaper took photos and recorded an interview before I put everything into the back of the lead reporter's car and they drove us back into the town. We went to the local Irish bar for a pint to celebrate. We all sat around eating Philly cheesesteak sandwiches, and I was drinking beer, all paid for by Pat, my WarmShowers host who I stayed with in the Outer Banks. It was so lovely of her to pay, and for her to be part of the final day of a three-year tour. Over lunch my parents asked me what I wanted to do: Did I want to cycle on to New York or did I want to call it a day here and come stay with them in their hotel? After three years, 46,500 kilometres and 39 countries I was done, and I went back with them to their hotel, took a nap and truly rested for the first time in three years!

*Epilogue*

I wanted to write something at the end to give the trip closure. A moment to reflect over those three years and see the overall effect of three years on a bicycle. My primary intention was to both explore with my own eyes and see if the world is a beautiful place. By travelling by bike I was able to see it all, the highlights and lowlights and it is only by being outside all the time was I truly able to explore. As for the world being a beautiful place, I can conclude that it truly is. The vast majority of the world and the people in it are wonderful, and after reading this book I can only hope you agree with me.

When being on a bike for three years it is impossible for that journey not to change you. To break the moulds in which you were held. You become someone else, you have experienced so much that those memories and experiences cannot help but shape you into the person you now are. I was changed irrevocably for the better. I had grown up and become more confident. I had overcome my initial fears and reservations about the world. I remember when I was scared of wild camping back in Europe, scared of the noises outside the tent. Now I could sleep anywhere, trusting that no harm would come to me. I had shown myself that I can complete big challenges and knew within myself that everyday I was on the right track to both the end point of the journey and the start of a new me.

Before I left I used to be quite anxious. I used to worry about what people thought of me but I masked this with trying my hardest to be very social, surrounding myself with friends. After the trip, I felt more confident, I felt like I had an identity and was finally on a path which made me both happy and content.

Upon coming home, it was fun to see everyone again. The first month involved many welcome home parties and reunions. It was amazing to see everyone again and was the perfect distraction from deciding what I was going to do next. It was also great to see Finola again, to reminisce with her about the trip. To reflect how amazing it was to have that experience together and knowing we will always have that bond and friendship.

I moved back into my parents house, since I had spent all the money I had saved on the trip, and I had to re-set myself financially. I was so lucky and grateful that they were able to put me up while I worked out my next steps. I knew my life lay in the outdoors and on adventures and I knew that I needed to change my career for the third time, from television production, to travel agent to outdoor guide.

I got a job with The Bushcraft Company, teaching bushcraft to children's groups in a beautiful protected woodland in Cornbury park, Oxfordshire. I loved being able to share my knowledge of the outdoors with the next generation. I feel it is so important to take children outside, away from their televisions and Wi-Fi and let them be kids in an outdoor setting. I would teach for 3–5 days a week and I was getting as much out of the experience as the children. I slept in my tent in the woods, enabling me to keep up an outdoor lifestyle throughout the summer and avoid the shock of going back into the 'normal' working world. I believe this helped me greatly avoid any post-trip depression as I went straight into something which was a similar experience to the cycle trip.

Following this, over the winter months, I moved to the middle east to teach stand-up paddleboarding and mountain biking in Qatar. This led to a summer back in England of bushcraft and speaking engagements: talking about all things cycling and adventure travel at festivals, corporate events, and adventure story-telling nights.

It was in 2019 when I also finally decided to write this book and took three months off work to pen the adventure. Something I never really thought would see the light of day but people kept encouraging me to do it. Writing about and reflecting on the journey was incredibly cathartic, and in publishing this book, a chapter of my life is finally closed. The best three years of my life so far.

What's next? Well, I am now lucky enough to get paid to work on bicycle expeditions all over the world and teaching bushcraft in the beautiful British woodland. I still have a yearning for big bicycle travel. I would like to cycle the Gibb

River Road in Western Australia and across Canada and Alaska. And Pakistan. And Iran. And walk some rivers in Venezuela... There's so much to cover.

But keep following me on social media and on my website as that is where all the latest news and updates will be shared.

timmillikin.com
instagram.com/timcmillikin
timcmillikin@gmail.com

Thank you for both purchasing and reading my book. It means so much that you invested your time and money to read about my little adventure. I hope you enjoyed it, and if you did can you please leave a review, as it really helps me get the book out there to a wider audience.

## Acknowledgements

Firstly I want to thank Finola: her determination and desire for adventure is half of what drove this trip in the first place.

I want to thank everyone who showed me kindness on the road. You were the trip, and meeting you and your families made the experience so real. It truly lives on in my memory and heart what warmth and generosity you showed me and I only wish I can repay you in kind one day. To those who are not included in the book, your memory is just as strong. I just did not have room for every person and every story.

I wish to thank all my family and friends for their constant support before, during and after these three years. Those I rode with and those at home. I know you were always looking out for me and I will never forget the messages, phone calls, donations and support you all showed me when I was in the hospital in El Salvador.

To the Jocoro police and the medical team in the San Miguel Hospital. You picked me up off the road and looked

290

after me when I was at my worst. To the medical team in the Xanxi hospital in China, you treated me like a guest not a patient and I recovered all the quicker for it.

To my team editors and proofreaders. Keidi Keating at yourbookangel, Ursula Martin, Cari Hook, Harry Gunn, Jenny Berkerley, Ian Preedy, Gemma Howes, Richard Collett, Lynsey Smith, Hiatt Zhao, Zoe Almond and Dan Bridle. Thank you, this book is better following your input.

Finally to the amazing Jo and Ann Lankester who worked with me tirelessly to polish, edit, read, and finish the book. It would not be the same without your input, although next time I promise we'll have more than two weeks to do it!